The White Umbrella

Walking with Survivors of Sex Trafficking

MARY FRANCES BOWLEY

MOODY PUBLISHERS

CHICAGO

Edited by James Lund and
Stephanie S. Smith of (In)dialogue Communications
Interior and Cover Design: Design Corps
Cover Images: is 8312404 / is 19697806 / is 13708083 /
        stock - illustration - 18632439
Author Photo: Melissa White

Library of Congress Cataloging-in-Publication Data

Bowley, Mary Frances.
 The white umbrella : walking with survivors of sex trafficking / Mary Frances Bowley.
    p. cm.
 Includes bibliographical references.
 ISBN 978-0-8024-0859-4
 1. Child trafficking. 2. Sexually abused girls. 3. Sexually abused children. I. Title.
 HQ281.B69 2012
 362.76—dc23

                                                2012028542

We hope you enjoy this book from Moody Publishers. Our goal is to provide high-quality, thought-provoking books and products that connect truth to your real needs and challenges. For more information on other books and products written and produced from a biblical perspective, go to www.moodypublishers.com or write to:

Moody Publishers
820 N. LaSalle Boulevard
Chicago, IL 60610

3 5 7 9 10 8 6 4 2

Printed in the United States of America

Praise for *The White Umbrella*

The White Umbrella will break your heart and inspire you to do something. Mary Frances Bowley is a modern day crusader and we view Wellspring Living as a strategic ministry partner.

—**ANDY STANLEY**, senior pastor, North Point Ministries

Too often followers of Jesus live as if they are casually unaware of the horrors of local and global sex trafficking. Our natural tendency is to be at ease within the walls of our churches, and we desperately need to be reminded of the brokenness that surrounds us every day. *The White Umbrella* wakes us to the urgent call for true gospel ministry to the innocent victims of this wickedness. Read and learn how to love these girls to restoration through the transforming power of Jesus Christ.

—**DR. JOHNNY M. HUNT**, president,
Southern Baptist Convention 2009–2010

In *The White Umbrella* Mary Frances Bowley brings names and stories to these shocking statistics. Her work with Wellspring Living has helped hundreds and inspired thousands to join the global movement of providing hope and restoration for those who have been freed from the oppression of modern day slavery. Read this book. Be inspired and DO SOMETHING NOW.

—**BRYSON VOGELTANZ**, pastor of Global Engagement,
Passion City Church/Passion Conferences

Mary Frances is a person who leads by doing. Her stories are rooted in the hard work of changing lives from sexually exploited to fully dignified individuals. I have seen her work firsthand and will forever be imprinted by this beautiful place of restoration. If you read this book, you will be learning from a national leader fighting for the dignity of women.

—**JEFF SHINABARGER**, founder and creative director of
Plywood People

The White Umbrella is a work of God's grace, just as each one of us is a work of God's grace. As you mull over these pages, I pray these writings inspire and mobilize you to rescue the perishing and care for the dying. That's exactly what these words did to Mary Frances when she decided to spend her life pouring into these young women . . . because they matter to Jesus.

—**BOYD BAILEY**, CEO of Ministry Ventures and president of
Wisdom Hunters

The White Umbrella is an important book to read. It's a necessary book to read. But at times, it's not an easy book to read. The real-life stories in here will break your heart but it will also move you to do something. This is what happened to my friend Mary Frances Bowley. These stories broke her heart and caused her to act by starting the incredible work of Wellspring Living. It's not a coincidence this book is now in your hands. Mary Frances and Wellspring need your help, and the best next step is for you to simply read *The White Umbrella*. But be prepared; no one can read this book and remain unmoved. Perhaps that's why you now have it in your hands.

—**JEFF HENDERSON**, lead pastor, Gwinnett Church,
   North Point Ministries

Finally, a book that articulates how the community of faith can move from empathy and sorrow for the soul victimized by abuse to a compassionate response to stand and serve confidently in their healing and spiritual transformation.

—**KAREN LORITTS**, speaker, author, former board member at
   Wellspring Living

Perhaps you know statistics of sexual exploitation, and if so, you likely can assume some of the sadness and horror. But you may never have heard actual stories of victims who have gone beyond the trauma into healing. You need to know these stories.

The White Umbrella will tell stories of trafficked women, but will also explain what happens practically in their very complex process of healing. You will learn how brain development is affected by trauma. You will be able to clearly see how recovery and healing always must come within the context of relationship and how that can happen. This is a book of profound hope.

With the rise in awareness of trafficking, it is easy to immediately feel a strong sense of justice yet not know how next to respond. *White Umbrella* describes multifaceted ways to practically respond. You can do something.

If God has drawn you to care for victims of sexual exploitation, this book is a first must-read.

—**PAMELA MacRAE**, assistant professor of Pastoral Studies,
   Moody Bible Institute

Dedicated to my Savior, Jesus Christ, who opened His covering of love and sacrifice so that I might experience a precious relationship with God.

To my best friend, Dick Bowley, who has supported the work of Wellspring Living since its inception.
He is my sounding board, my prayer warrior, and the love of my life!

To every compassionate person who has been willing to open your life to a hurting person and walk beside him or her.

To Martha Jeane Giglio, who embodied the life of an intercessor for Wellspring Living.
Martha Jeane's dedication through prayer was and continues to be an inspiration to me.

To every girl or woman who has experienced sexual abuse and exploitation and has had the courage to walk through recovery. May this book encourage you to allow the umbrella of God's love and caring people to strengthen you for the rest of your life.

Contents

A Note from the Author

All of the stories in this book are true. Many of the names and a few minor details have been altered to protect the girls we serve.

Profits from the sales of *The White Umbrella* will go directly to Wellspring Living to further its work in confronting the issue of childhood sexual abuse and exploitation through awareness, training, and treatment for girls and women. Wellspring Living strategies include:

- Offering survivors a safe haven where they receive therapy, personalized education, life skills, and spiritual renewal
- Advocating for victims—to give a voice to the voiceless and confront the issue of sexual exploitation
- Sharing best practices with others by training organizations to assist in building programs that serve survivors of childhood sexual abuse and exploitation

Wellspring Living desires to embody servant leadership, unrelenting compassion, community mindedness, comprehensive service, excellent care, and strong faith.

white ('hwīt, 'wīt) adj.

Free from spot or blemish as (1) free from moral impurity:
INNOCENT (2) marked by the wearing of white by the woman
as a symbol of purity.

um·brel·la (əm-'bre-lə) n.

1. A device for protection from the weather consisting of a
collapsible, usually circular canopy mounted on a central rod.
2. Something that covers or protects.

Foreword

Life on planet earth is not as it should be. I don't think anyone reading these words will argue that assumption. Though imagined and created by a beautiful and perfect Creator, our lives and our world have been ravished by the damaging effects of our fallen pride. As a result, we each navigate our days in a broken planet, one that leaves innocent people marginalized and wounded, victims of the brutality and abuse of others. One specific result of the mayhem is the staggering number of women and girls who are bought and sold each day under the ruthless control of others and for their captors' financial gain.

In fact, as you will discover within these pages, not only are women and girls being bought and sold, chances are it's happening a lot closer than you think to where you are right now.

While accepting that shattered lives surround us, too often we give in to the false notion that one person can't really make a huge difference in such a messed-up world. This weak rationalization, most likely nothing more than a cover-up for our selfish ways, fashions the blinders that protect our eyes and keep our hands clean. As long as we are convinced that "somebody like me" can't really do anything to turn the tide, we can continue to exist in our self-made bubbles of comfort and ignore God's beating heart. Yet throughout history, in the dark night of need, God awakens ordinary people to the torrent of His love, shattering the silence and fueling in their hearts an unquenchable desire to spread the love they've found to the broken and discarded. One such warrior of love is my friend Mary Frances Bowley. While many regard Mary Frances as a hero (an apt description), what I really want you to know about her is that she is someone just like you. She's what you'd call a "normal" person who was living a comfortable "Christian" life until the very real plight of sexual slavery stood right in front of her with a face and a name.

In that moment, everything changed for Mary Frances; and from that moment she has set out to change everything. As you'll read, Mary Frances went on to found Wellspring Living, a fledgling dream of hope that has now blossomed into a nationally recognized titan force of rescue, restoration, and renewal for lives once torn.

I first came to know about Wellspring Living from my mom, Martha Jeane Giglio. A legendary intercessor, Mom would always tell me about the young women she met while leading devotions at the home run by Mary Frances's organization. Though she protected the details of their stories, she would tell our family she was praying for certain girls, believing God for their healing even when the young women weren't ready to take that stand for their own lives. Mom wrote all their names and prayer requests in a spiral notebook she kept by her bed. Toward the end of her life on earth, when hospital stays became frequent, she always wanted to make sure we'd grab her Bible and that notebook and bring them along. One night, a day or so after fairly serious surgery, I walked into Mom's hospital room and found her holding the notebook open to a page where a young woman had written her prayer requests in her own handwriting. Mom's eyes were closed and she was lost in heaven contending for a precious young lady before the throne of grace and mercy of God.

God's heart breaks for the 27 million men, women, and children worldwide who are trapped in some form of slavery. It's horrifying and absurd to think that there are currently more slaves on earth than at any other time in human history. But once that massive number overwhelms your heart, take a step back and consider that each one of them has a face and a name. While it may be impossible for any one of us to reach and rescue every one of them, each one of us can certainly make a difference in one precious life.

Slavery must end, and it must end now. Fortunately, the solutions are not beyond our reach. They just require that you raise your White Umbrella of hope and action right where you are. Together, we can be and will be a force for good, a sea of freedom fighters blanketing the world with the blinding light of His great love.

Mary Frances has paved the way for us all; so lean forward and let her story propel and guide you as you raise your voice for freedom and liberty for all. As there is for her and for my mom and for me, there is a place for you in this fight.

Louie Giglio
Pastor, Passion City Church, Atlanta

The Story behind the White Umbrella

You hear the terms. *Sex trafficking. Human trafficking. Sex trade. Sexual slavery.* If you think about it at all, you figure it's something that goes on in places like India, Cambodia, Russia, and Latin America. Not anywhere close to home. Not here.

Sadly, you are wrong.

The FBI reports that in the United States, the number of children, usually girls, who are forced to do someone's sexual bidding is well over 100,000. The age range is nine to nineteen. The average age is just eleven years old.[1]

Some of these kids are runaways and some are abandoned. Many others come from "good" homes. They are the victims of cruel and clever predators who know just what to offer—the appearance of friendship, a listening ear, the promise of love or money or a new life.

Some girls are even lured from their own driveways. That's what happened to Debbie, a fifteen-year-old from Phoenix who earned straight As at school. One minute she was talking to a casual friend just outside her house. The next minute, the "friend" and two men were pushing Debbie into a car, where she was bound and gagged. She was held captive for more than forty days and forced to have sex with several men daily until a tip led to her rescue.[2]

We're talking about Americans kidnapping Americans. How can this be happening to our friends, sisters, and daughters? It's outrageous, disgusting, and frightening. It's also big business. Worldwide, the sex trade generates an estimated $32 billion in income each year. It is second behind only the drug industry as the world's leading criminal enterprise.[3] It is what the FBI calls an epidemic.[4]

Sex trafficking isn't just going on "out there" somewhere. It's happening in your state. Maybe even your town.

And it's time we did something about it.

For most of my years, I was completely unaware of the sexual slave trade and the desperate lives of so many young women. I was a mom, wife, and kindergarten and Bible teacher, with no aspirations to do anything outside my bubble of a life in Peachtree City, Georgia, the golf cart capitol of the South. But in 1993, all that changed. A gentleman in my church told me about a local hairdresser who needed help. Sara was dealing with a desperate family situation and couldn't handle it alone. I decided to talk to Sara, to get to know her, to show her I cared. *I'll buy her a Christian book,* I thought. *She'll read it and understand that God loves her. That will make things better.*

But as I got to know Sara and her struggles, I realized that nothing I'd encountered prepared me to help her put back together the pieces of her broken life. I'd grown up in a strong Christian home and attended every church activity on the calendar—choir practices, mission programs, vacation Bible schools. My background didn't qualify me to help her "fix" it.

Now *I* was the desperate one. What was I supposed to do?

That's when God stepped in. Though I wouldn't have described it like this at the time, He was introducing me to a new idea: the white umbrella.

An umbrella is a common item, usually left forgotten in the back of a closet until needed. But when nature delivers a downpour or hailstorm, an umbrella makes a difference—a buffer that protects us from the harsh elements falling from the sky. An umbrella often does something else as well—it brings those who suffer together. When you share one with someone, you have to stand close, side by side.

That's what I needed to do for Sara. I needed to share my "umbrella" by standing close and providing cover as best I could. Some weeks that meant spending time with her daughters. Other times it meant bringing meals or offering transportation. I learned that helping Sara wasn't about a formula for fixing her or her situation; it was simply about being available to stand with her during the storms of life, letting her know that I was there—and that God was there too.

Soon my eyes were opened to the plight of many more young women who were struggling against the storms. So many girls, I discovered, grew up in homes marked by emotional, physical, and sexual abuse. These girls were hurting. They were in despair. They'd lost hope.

They needed cover. They needed a chance.

I knew I couldn't help them all. I knew I couldn't do it alone. I wasn't sure we could help any of them. But maybe, I thought, we could make a small difference for a few. Or even one. Just one.

As unlikely as it seemed, these vague ideas turned into a passion that would not let me go. I prayed about it. I talked with other women from our church. I talked with everyone I knew. Soon, I was joining with forty other women who shared a desire to reach beyond the walls of our church to try to help young women in need. We decided to call our nonprofit program Wellspring Living, after the living water Jesus promised to the Samaritan woman at the well.

That was over a decade ago. Today, Atlanta-based Wellspring Living serves as a recovery home for adult survivors of childhood sexual abuse, an outpatient counseling center, and a safe place for women escaping from unsafe situations as they look for new options.

And, since 2008, we have offered a program for child survivors of forced prostitution and sex trafficking. Throughout this book, you will notice that I often refer to the clients we work with as "girls." This is because, regardless of literal age, the children and women who come to Wellspring Living are all wounded little girls inside. Once a girl is molested, she is emotionally arrested at that age, making her vulnerable to unhealthy people and giving her a tendency of making life choices based on the age at abuse. We also refer to them often as "our girls" out of the great love, respect, and community we are privileged to share with them day to day.

The foundation of what we do is our network of volunteers—we wouldn't exist without them. Somewhere near you is a program similar to Wellspring Living that needs *your* help. There are a thousand ways to get involved. You can drive a girl to a doctor appointment. You can teach her how to cook. You can donate clothes, furniture, or money. You can pray for her and with her. You can simply listen and treat her with love and respect. For her, it may be an entirely new experience.

My heart aches for these girls. So many have been battered, bruised, and abused. They have weathered storms few of us can imagine. They are often suspicious of relationships and offered help. They do not smile or trust easily. They have been betrayed too many times. To survive, they have learned to be tough. Yet underneath the hard exterior is the loving person God intended them to be.

Who will help these young women stand against the storms? I believe it's up to you and me.

To me, a white umbrella is the perfect symbol. The color white represents purity—the purity these girls still possess and the motivation we have, without any agenda, to help them recover it. Our volunteers respect these young ladies as people. They look beneath the surface to glimpse the person God created them to be. Part of our call is portraying their innocence and worth to others who might not believe in them.

The umbrella represents protection against the storms and our willingness to stand with these girls shoulder to shoulder. Girls who have been trafficked live in a whirlwind of chaos and crisis. Like a tornado, you can't understand it unless you're in it. Our courageous volunteers and staff hold an umbrella over these young women, providing cover and letting them know they're not alone.

This book tells the stories of girls who are victims of the dark underworld of sex trafficking and of the volunteers and caregivers who try to cover them with the love of Jesus. More importantly, it shows what you can do to help.

Being involved is hard. It is a journey with many twists and turns. More than an adventure, it is a quest—a calling that does not allow you to return to normal, humdrum life. A calling that beckons you to step outside your comfortable bubble to reach out to those who are desperate in the storm.

Are you ready to embark on the quest of your life? If so, I invite you to open and share your white umbrella of grace and love.

01~ Her Story

What goes on in the mind of a child who has suffered abuse and abandonment? How is she enticed into the sleazy sphere of sex trafficking? How does she survive? How can we reach out to her? Shelia's story is our first glimpse into that world.

As hard as I try, I can't forget that first night. I was seven years old. I'd put on my Princess Ariel pajamas and brushed my teeth. I'd climbed into bed with my white stuffed pony, the one I always slept with, the one my dad had given me two years before when my parents split up. I knew my mom wouldn't come to say good night because she was on a business trip. So it didn't surprise me when Brad, my stepdad, came to my room instead.

But I was surprised, and scared, when he turned off the light and crawled under the covers with me. "Shelia, we're going to play a game," he said.

Only it wasn't a game.

Brad began touching me in places he wasn't supposed to touch. I didn't understand what was happening. I was confused and too scared to say anything. Brad was so much bigger than me, and he had a temper.

When he finished, he made me promise to not tell anyone about our "game." If I did, he said, he'd hurt my mom and Sarah, my little sister. I believed him.

For the rest of my elementary school years and into middle school, the game continued. The only way I got through those nights was to think about something else. It only happened when my mom was gone or out of town. She never suspected a thing.

Outside of my home, I lived a normal life. I made good grades, played sports, and had a few close friends. But on the inside, I felt dirty and worthless. I felt like I needed to hide. Sometimes I wanted to die.

If anyone had paid attention, they might have noticed how the light in my face had been extinguished. I never laughed and rarely smiled. I swayed back and forth between screaming inside for attention and help, and not wanting to be known at all. How would I know if a person was safe? How could I ever trust again? Mom was gone a lot, and even when she was home, she fought with Brad most of the time. She didn't seem to have much energy for me.

By the time I was twelve years old, the chaos and pain were too much. I couldn't take it anymore. I was sure there had to be something better outside the walls of my home. I was worried about Sarah, but I had to get away from Brad. I thought I could find someone who would care for me, someone who saw value in me. I ran away.

The Nicest Man

Suddenly, I was alone. I had no food and no place to sleep. But it wasn't long before I met the nicest guy. He bought me a cheeseburger at McDonald's. I was so hungry I ate three of them.

The man's name was Michael. He wore a heavy jacket and a blue stocking cap. He was a big man, but he had a soft voice, not like Brad's at all.

"Shelia, you don't seem like the other girls I see on that street," he said. "You're pretty and you seem really smart. How did you end up out here?"

Before I knew it, I was telling Michael everything about me. I'd finally met someone I could open up to, someone who understood me. He seemed to know that I needed someone like him to take care of me. He offered a place to stay. I couldn't believe it. I actually had someone I could trust to help me. I didn't have to stay silent and scared anymore.

Michael took me to a fancy townhome. There were seven other girls my age there. I thought, *This is like a boarding place for girls who need help*. I never noticed that the doors were bolted from the outside.

Around 10 p.m., Michael said he and the other girls needed to go out for a while. He told me to make myself at home. I made a peanut butter and jelly sandwich and sat down to watch TV. It felt great to be alone and safe.

About thirty minutes later, the front door opened. Three men staggered in, laughing. "Well, hi there, honey," one said. His words were friendly, but his voice was not. These men made me nervous. Something didn't seem right.

My instinct was correct. All of a sudden, one of the men grabbed me by the arm and roughly steered me into a bedroom. Before I knew what was happening, they pushed me onto the bed and held me down. They pulled my clothes off. Then they raped me repeatedly.

A few minutes later, I was alone and shaking. *What is happening to me?* I thought. *This can't be real.* Finally, I got the courage to get my clothes on and start moving. I had to get out of there, get back to the streets. But when I tried to open the door, nothing happened. I realized it was locked from the other side.

I was trapped.

An Unending Circus

When Michael returned later, it was as if the night had turned him into a different person. It turned out he wasn't nice at all. He told me that I would have to "earn my keep," that this was the way it worked in his world. He would take me to a place, and I would service every man who walked into the room. My life was spinning out of control.

The next night, Michael put me and the seven other girls into a van. Sure enough, he dropped each girl off at a different place. I noticed that each time a girl entered a house or apartment, a man stood guard just outside the door.

I was the last one to be left. The apartment was dark and smelled of sweat and smoke. In just a few minutes, a man entered, and I did what he said. I had no choice. The scene was repeated again and again. I don't even know how many men came in that night. The only way I could endure the pain was by thinking about something else, just like I did with Brad. At the end of the night, which was actually morning, Michael picked me up. He said I'd done well, that I'd brought in a thousand dollars. I was relieved. Maybe, I thought, this would be the only time I'd have to live through a nightmare like this.

I was wrong. The next night it was the same scenario, and the night after that, and the night after that. The circus was unending. Most of the time, I had little to eat. To make sure we were "productive," Michael put drugs in our drinks. The drugs made us stay awake for days at a time. It all seemed to go on forever. Nights turned into weeks, weeks into months.

About five months later, on a Tuesday night, I was dropped off at a different apartment. I went in and began to prepare myself to separate my mind from what was about to happen. There was a knock on the door. It was Sanchez, the man who always stood guard to make sure I didn't run away.

"Our first customer is late," he said.

Suddenly I was alone at the apartment. In the early days, I'd fantasized many times about escaping, but there had always been someone watching. Besides, where would I go? Michael and Sanchez would find me and probably kill me. Before long I'd given up hope of ever getting away.

But now, unexpectedly, there was a chance. I checked the locks in the apartment, barely daring to hope, when I discovered the bathroom window was unlocked. I remembered seeing a fire station a couple of blocks away from the apartment. It hadn't meant anything then, but now I wondered. Could I really do it? Would they be able to protect me? Could I get there without being seen?

I climbed on the toilet and was able to squeeze through the window. My heart hammered so loud I was sure someone would hear or see me. My fear mounting with each step, I found myself walking to the entrance of the complex and into the street.

Once I reached the sidewalk, I broke into a run. It was the longest two blocks I'd ever covered. Finally, though, I reached the firehouse and pounded on the door. When a man in a blue fire department uniform answered, I burst into tears.

"Please help me!" I cried.

I don't know exactly what I expected, but the "help" they provided wasn't what I'd hoped for. I ended up spending that night at a youth detention center. I remember walking into a cold, dark place with bars all around. Concrete walls and grey concrete floors surrounded me. After I was "processed," I was taken to my room. It was so small. The bed was made of metal and had a thin, green, plastic cushion. There was a metal chair and metal sink and metal toilet and metal mirror. I was alone again, in the dark. My life had gone from bad to worse.

Is This What Love Feels Like?

After being in jail for about five days, a lady came to "evaluate" me. She asked a lot of questions. She told me that what had happened to me wasn't my fault, and that I could go to a home where I would be safe, go to school, and get counseling. I thought, *I wasn't born yesterday. Everyone who's said they have something good for me has only used me.*

After the woman left, I continued to think about what she said. Even though I didn't want to take the chance on going somewhere new, I didn't want to stay in jail. What if I got out? Michael would surely find me. These last few days were the first I'd slept and eaten in a long time. The more I thought about my options, the more I thought maybe I should try this place.

So that Friday I was taken to the home and introduced to the staff. They seemed nice, but I kept up my guard. I would have my own room and bathroom. The rooms were nice, but so was the first townhome my trafficker took me to. Could I trust them?

> I had never known anyone who would do something for me without asking for something in return. It was like a dream.

That first month, I resisted everyone's attempts to reach out to me. I'm glad they didn't push themselves on me, but gave me room to get to know them and get comfortable in my new setting.

One thing that surprised me was that they worked hard to determine my past school credits and helped me create a plan to catch up on all I'd missed by being out of school for months. I found out later that they did this for each girl in the home. Each girl gets to choose what subjects she wants to work on and the teachers and volunteers help everyone stay on track.

Soon I met Becky, my counselor. She began to help me talk through everything that had happened to me. She helped me understand what I was truly created for. She believed that I was a person of value. In fact, everyone there seemed to think I was a great person. No one had ever had confidence in me. No one had ever been so patient with me. I had never known anyone who would do something for me without asking for something in return. It was like a dream.

Before long I was again excelling in school. I began to think there might be something to this program.

I kept waiting for things to change for the worse, like they always had in my life. But day after day, I encountered people who seemed to really care about me and believe in me. It wasn't just the staff. There were so many volunteers who came in each day either to help me with my classes or teach me something cool or help me dream about a career or maybe college someday.

Is this what love feels like? I wondered.

I pondered this question a lot. I knew there was something unusual about these people. They were different from any people I'd ever met. They all seemed to believe in God, but they didn't use a lot of "churchy" words. They just cared for me whether I was in a good mood or not, whether I made an A on a test or not, and whether I responded to their love or not. I hadn't thought much about God before. I didn't know if I believed in Him. But I started thinking it might be time to find out.

While I was in the program, I changed from a girl who was shy, scared, and silent to a girl who had learned to express herself, laugh out loud, and become confident in herself. I reconnected with my mom, who'd divorced Brad, and with Sarah. Months went by, and my graduation date approached. One of the volunteers asked if she could be my mentor when I left the program. I really couldn't believe that! A person who was a stranger months ago now wanted to spend time with me.

I don't know what the future holds for me, and I still have occasional nightmares about my past. Sometimes it's still hard to trust people. But I'm working on it day by day. I can only say that my life is different because so many people reached out to me and believed in me. I know now that I'm not worthless—and that life just might be worth living again (www.thewhiteumbrellacampaign.com/video/#Everything).

02~ They're Still Little Girls

Every girl who enters Wellspring Living
has had innocence stolen from her. To
survive, each had learned to be tough,
brave, and strong. When we tear down
the walls created by trauma and abuse,
however, we find what remains is the heart
of a little girl. Tracy Busse, our clinical
director, shares a few glimpses of these
innocent souls, along with the story of
her own journey to Wellspring Living.

by Tracy Busse

Who knew that a vacation to Idaho would further open my eyes to the world of commercial and sexual exploitation of children? In 2008, I was a substance abuse counselor for the state of Georgia, working with addicts and juvenile sex offenders. By that summer, I was more than ready for a vacation, so I visited a friend in the Northwest, which led us to the Oasis Bordello Museum in Wallace, Idaho.

When I entered the dark, saloon-style structure, I thought I was looking at ancient history, a bordello from the 1800s old West. Yet when we started the tour, our guide, a little lady in her eighties, revealed that this bordello was still operating as late as 1988, closing only after the women inside fled in a panic during an FBI investigation into gambling that year.

We climbed rickety stairs to reach a kitchen area. A case of diet soda, boxes of macaroni and cheese, and a bag of Doritos had been left just as they were that last night. On the wall was a list of "services," complete with prices and timed to the minute. "Eight minutes, fifteen dollars, straight, no frills," read one. Farther down a dark, narrow hallway, we found bedrooms littered with cans of hair spray and boxes of press-on nails, as well as mannequins dressed in lingerie to represent the women who populated these shadowy corners.

It was worse than cheesy. It was disgusting.

I looked closer at some of the items in the bedrooms, which included video games and Care Bears. I listened to our guide tell how some of the women who had sold their bodies here had returned recently to see the museum. When she mentioned their current ages, I did the math. They weren't women when they lived here, having sex every night with locals and out-of-towners. They were kids, probably no more than fifteen or sixteen.

My heart sank as I imagined these children "working" at the bordello. Did any of them feel they had a choice? How does this happen? How could the men and women of this town allow it? Why did I just pay three dollars to go through this so-called museum?

I was angry and sick to my stomach. I had no idea that the world of the bordello would soon invade my own.

I didn't realize it at the time of my visit to the Idaho bordello, but God was nudging me toward a new awareness of sexual exploitation of children. Soon after, I watched a powerful documentary on human trafficking. Then I counseled a teen boy who'd been forced to watch pornography with his parents at the age of seven. A few months later, two friends emailed to tell me about an opening for a therapist at Wellspring Living.

I was ready for a change and applied for the position, but I didn't expect anything to come of it. The commute was too far, the pay was too low, and the benefits didn't come close to what I had. When Wellspring called me about an interview, however, I went. At the interview, I was handed a book by Wellspring's director, Mary Frances Bowley. The title was *A League of Dangerous Women*.[5]

When I saw it, I swallowed hard. For years I'd been praying that God would show me how to be more "dangerous" for Him. This was one of the core desires of my life. Was He trying to tell me something?

Even so, I didn't think I could accept the job if it was offered. My biggest, practical objection was the salary. I decided I'd better pray about it. As I did, I sensed the Lord giving me a number, a salary that I *could* live on. I wrote it down.

Less than an hour later, my phone rang. It was Jenn McEwen, Wellspring's vice president. "Tracy, we're really interested in offering you this position," she said. "I know salary is an issue for you, so we've decided to increase the amount we can offer." When she shared the number, tears came to my eyes. It was the exact same figure I'd written down.

My voice cracked a little when I said, "Yes, I accept." I wasn't just saying yes to a job offer, a new salary, and professional growth. I was saying yes to God's call and mission for my life.

Today, I am clinical director of Wellspring Living Girls' Program. I oversee our clinical program, develop new programs, speak in the community about what we do, serve on committees that promote awareness and prevention of sexual exploitation, and still counsel a few of the girls. I love it. I'm excited every morning about going in to work.

When I was in college, I felt the Lord pointing me to Isaiah 61:1 as my life's calling, which reads, "He has sent me to bind up the brokenhearted, to proclaim freedom for the captives." It reminds me that a couple of the girls at Wellspring love swing sets. They get on them whenever they can. One of them once said to me, "When I swing, I feel like I'm free."

That's what I try to do today—to help each and every one of these special girls find freedom.

Simple Comforts

Kalina was seventeen when I met her. She'd just entered the Wellspring Living Girls' Program after surviving three years of being sold for sex. Her mother didn't *force* Kalina into a life of sexual exploitation—she just introduced her to a pimp and made it clear she wasn't allowed to come home unless she helped pay the bills. Even so, Kalina still desperately wanted her mother's love and approval. After Kalina joined us, we scheduled a weekly family therapy session for her and her mother. And every week, Kalina was disappointed when her mom didn't show up.

On one of these days, Kalina and I sat in the family room near the front door of the Wellspring home. The time for the appointment came and went. Fifteen minutes passed, then twenty. I pulled out my cell phone.

"Kalina, I don't think your mom is coming," I said. "She's not answering her phone."

Silent tears ran down Kalina's face. She'd had her heart broken one time too many. She got up, went to her room, and returned with a small, white teddy bear. Kalina is tall and looks older than her years, but on this day she didn't seem old at all. She curled into a fetal position on the couch next to me, clung to her teddy bear, and cried.

Laughter in Unlikely Places

The sex industry has many dark and tragic corners, but it shows how big our God is when He is pleased to shine His light—and even humor—through it.

Candice was thirteen when a man in his thirties—her pimp—had convinced her that he was her boyfriend. It took time and a lot of counseling for her to begin to see that this guy didn't love her, that he was using her. Even then, Candice was sometimes confused and conflicted over her feelings about him.

The day came when Candice needed to testify in court against this man, a traumatic experience for anyone. To help her prepare, we had a long and intense conversation about it. At the end of our talk, as Candice was ready to leave, she turned to me. I expected her to ask something about how the court system works or what the prosecutor would say, or even bring up that she was having second thoughts about testifying. Instead, she said, "Miss Tracy, after we go, can we stop for McDonald's fries on the way home?" It reminded me that even though she was facing some very tough and grown-up circumstances, she was still barely a teenager.

Candice did testify, and afterward, we did stop for those fries. She devoured them. With a big smile on her face, she repeated a marketing slogan she'd heard: "Check the bottom of the bag; remember, there's always one left." I couldn't help laughing.

Serena was another girl in our program who made me laugh—but not at first.

Both of Serena's parents were drug addicts. The state took custody of her and put her in foster homes, but Serena kept running away and was eventually lured into the world of sex trafficking. At age sixteen, she was arrested for prostitution (Georgia state law no longer allows minors to be prosecuted for prostitution) and placed in the Wellspring Living Girls' Program.

One day I was sitting in my office and heard a series of high-pitched moans. *What is that terrible noise?* When I got up to investigate, I found Serena on all fours with Cool Joe, a brown lab who was part of our dog therapy program. These dogs are brought in once a week to interact with the girls and show them safe, unconditional love. Serena was on the floor surrounded by a crowd of girls. She moaned loudly in Cool Joe's face.

"Serena, what are you doing?" I asked.

"I'm trying to get him to howl!"

She kept at it, even though the rest of us couldn't help laughing at her. But it worked. Pretty soon Cool Joe let loose with one howl after another. Serena sat up, clapped her hands, and beamed. Then she joined in, making it a duet.

It was one of the most awful—and wonderful—sounds I'd ever heard.

Permission to Play

Jada was a tough seventeen-year-old. She never knew her father. Her mother was unsupportive. She'd been exploited in multiple cities. Once her pimp lured her into his home, beat her, and locked her in, forcing her to live and "work" there for the next three months. She escaped and lived on the street for a year, still selling her body to make enough money to eat.

When Jada entered Wellspring, she was hard and full of anger. She frequently got into fights with the other girls. One day I noticed Jada arguing with someone and getting increasingly frustrated.

"Jada," I said, "will you come outside with me?"

We stepped into the yard. "What are we doing out here?" she said. I led her to my car. I opened my trunk and showed her all the junk I kept there. One item caught her attention.

"What's that?" she said.

"It's a kite." The kite was an orange-and-yellow blowfish, with a comical mouth and wide, rolling eyes.

"What do you do with it?"

"You fly it."

We took the kite out. Jada spent the next half hour running through the yard, dragging the kite behind her. She couldn't get it into the air, but it did help her release the anger that had boiled up inside. Then I explained how to pull the kite into the wind. Once she got that blowfish to fly, Jada laughed and squealed like a little girl.

A few minutes later, she walked over to me. "Miss Tracy," she said, "when we were inside, I was about to get in a fight. I would have got arrested and I didn't care. How did you know to come play with me?"

Restoring a Sense of Worth

A friend once dragged me to a club for what we thought would be country line dancing. It was college night, open to anyone eighteen and older, though many didn't look even that old. Techno beats were pounding, kids were grinding, and I kept wondering when the country music would start. It never did. It was also bikini night, so of course the club had set up pedestals for the girls to dance on. I watched in sadness as young girls gyrated on these miniature stages while boys and older men alike stared. A girl would step down and walk away alone. The guys would move to the next pedestal and dancing girl.

It was obvious that these girls had ceased to be people in the eyes of these guys. They'd become sexual objects to gawk at.

We talk often with the girls at Wellspring Living about how women and even young girls are portrayed as objects in the media. It's another way that our society robs girls of their innocence. Movies, TV shows, magazines, and the Internet bombard us with images of women in sexual poses, surrounded by men, the women often so covered with makeup that they resemble a doll more than a person.

We also talk with our girls about the meaning of the phrase "the normalization of sexual harm," as well as different definitions of love, including the *agape* love described in the Bible. It helps the girls understand that their pimps don't actually love them as people but only for what the girls can do for them.

This, in turn, leads us into discussions about value. "How much are you worth?" I ask them. "Fifty dollars? Three hundred dollars?" We try to help the girls see that they are not objects to be bought and sold. That they have value beyond measure. That they are priceless.

Redefining Our Vision

As an avid follower of the Chicago Cubs, I have adopted the motto of Cubs fans around the globe: we believe. It's been over one hundred years since the Cubs have won a World Series, but no matter how horrible the Cubs are, we will always believe.

Not so long ago, if you had asked me if I thought it was possible to overcome the issue of sexual exploitation of children, I would have said no. I would've told you we can save individual lives but that only the return of Jesus would make the problem go away entirely. Recently I was challenged by the Lord to think bigger.

We often refer to human trafficking as modern-day slavery. I wondered—did African Americans enslaved in the 1800s think they would be free someday? Did it cross their minds that it was possible to overcome slavery in America?

Obviously some *did* believe. But who got the ball rolling? Was it a man in the fields, crying out to God for freedom? Was it a young mother praying for a better future for her children? Was it a citizen wondering how people could treat other human beings like animals? My guess is that God faithfully answered the prayers of many.

Today, I sense the Lord calling me to believe that one day people will look back on our fight to free sexually exploited children as history, not as reality. The Holy Spirit is prodding my heart to stand strong on the battle lines because one day we will see an end to trafficking.

In her beautiful song written for those who battle against trafficking, Sara Groves sings, "Ain't no man on earth control the weight of glory on a human soul."[6] When God's people come together to fight this good fight against the exploitation of innocence, the weight of oppression is exchanged for the weight of glory. The time has come to let our children be little girls once again. The time for freedom is now.

03~ We All Can Do Something

Not all of us are experts in treating and counseling victims of sexual abuse and trafficking. But we all can do something. The smallest gesture can make a lasting difference in the life of a hurting young woman. Sandy Kimbrough is one woman who is changing lives through the simplest of gifts-a willingness to share her time and encouragement.

by Sandy Kimbrough

The first time I laid eyes on Jessica, I could see she was hurting. She was sixteen, a cute girl, tall and slender, with dark skin, and hair dyed a flaming red. A cheerleader type, I thought. Except Jessica wasn't leading any cheers that day. She sat at her table with her head down.

Jessica was one of the girls in my cooking and nutrition classes at Wellspring Living. I'd just signed on as a volunteer, and though I didn't have a lot of skills to help these girls, I did know how to cook. I figured this was one small way I could make a difference.

I wasn't sure how I was going to make a difference for Jessica, though. She was closed up, like a flower afraid to bloom. After the last class of each week, I made it a habit to sit down with the girls and plan our menus for the next week. When I asked what they wanted, many piped up with suggestions—favorite dishes, comfort food, anything they craved. But not Jessica; she never said a word.

"Jessica," I once asked, in a simple attempt to draw her out, "would you prefer meatballs or chicken in your sauce?"

Her answer, head still down, was barely audible: "Doesn't matter."

There weren't a lot of things that mattered to Jessica, because for most of her young life, what she wanted didn't matter to anyone. She just had to live through whatever came at her next.

Living in a Nightmare

Jessica was born in Louisiana, but she didn't stay there long. In fact, she never stayed anywhere long. Her mother moved constantly, stringing Jessica's childhood through different towns, cities, and states. Jessica didn't know her father at all. She saw him just once. Because they never put down roots, Jessica never had things that are staples in most homes—a room of her own, a mattress. For a time, she and her mother were even homeless. Jessica's mom did what she could to bring in a few dollars. Sometimes her mother brought a man home for the night. Some nights she didn't come home at all.

They moved to Atlanta when Jessica was ten. Soon after, her mother left her with a nineteen-year-old male babysitter named Ervin. It was the beginning of a nightmare. Ervin molested her sexually, then threatened to hurt her if she ever told anyone. Confused and scared, Jessica kept quiet. The abuse continued for the next two years.

When Jessica was twelve, her drug-addicted mother disappeared. It was not unusual for her mother to not come back at night, but this time she did not come back at all. Jessica didn't know what to do. Ervin told her how she could make some cash. He introduced her to an old man. Desperate and knowing she needed money to survive, she agreed to sleep with him.

Ervin soon became Jessica's pimp. He controlled who she had sex with and when, where she lived, and the money she earned. It was a miserable life for a young girl, but Jessica saw no options. She had no family or friends to help her. She was trapped.

In 2010, when Jessica was fifteen, the nightmare took an even darker turn. A "client" who Ervin arranged for her turned out to be an undercover policeman. She was arrested and put in a juvenile detention facility—all for a crime she never wanted to commit. The judge gave her two choices: jail or a program for young women called Wellspring Living. Scared and numb, she chose the program. Anything to stay out of jail.

What Do I Have to Offer?

I understood why Jessica had so much trouble trusting me and the other volunteers and caregivers at Wellspring. She had to be wondering what we could say or do that would make any difference.

I admit that I sometimes wondered the same thing. I'd grown up in a strong Christian home and now was over fifty years old. How could I relate to these girls? Would they accept me? Did I have anything to offer them at all?

My doubts intensified on one of my first days of teaching at Wellspring. Some of the girls were quizzing me about hip-hop artists. Because my youngest son is a hip-hop musician, I knew a few of the names, but most I'd never heard of.

"Well," one girl named Latisha concluded, "when someone gets old and fat like you, I guess you kind of lose touch." I sensed the girls were suddenly watching me intently. How would I respond?

Latisha's comment wasn't something I wanted to hear, but before I got angry or upset, I thought about what was really going on. I might be old compared to these girls, but I was *not* fat. Latisha was testing me. She was probing to see if I would burn her like so many others had done before. Was I really there to help or would I turn on her at the first opportunity?

So instead of snapping back, I tried to make a joke. "That's why I wear this," I said, pointing to my long, loose blouse, "to cover up *this*." I pinched my waist.

Latisha didn't know what to make of my reply. But it obviously made an impression. Two weeks later, she approached me with worry lines etched onto her young face. "Miss Sandy, I'm so sorry," she said. "I didn't mean what I said about you. Will you forgive me?"

"Oh, honey," I answered. "I forgave you when you said it." Then Latisha hugged me for the very first time.

It seemed Latisha was beginning to trust me. But I wondered if Jessica would ever let me into her world.

In cooking class, it pained me to watch Jessica shut down when anyone tried to talk to her. Every time she shrugged, it was as if she withdrew deeper into herself. But the eating table has a way of opening people up.

I thought my continued efforts to reach out to Jessica weren't making much difference until one day, when I walked into the classroom and Jessica was waiting for me. "Miss Sandy," she said, "can we make pancakes today?"

By the end of our class that day, we were all splattered with pancake batter and sticky with syrup, and I saw Jessica smile for the first time. No comfort food could have hit the spot better than that.

The cooking classes ended, and I switched to a new volunteer position with Wellspring, purchasing office and school supplies. I didn't see much of Jessica or the other girls from those classes, but I missed them and wondered how they were doing. Finally, I decided to do something about it.

Christmas with the Girls

I've always loved the Christmas season and the chance to celebrate the birth of Jesus with family and other loved ones. I enjoy decorating our home for the holidays. But I realized that all of this is a luxury not many of the Wellspring girls get to enjoy, so I decided to share some of that joy with them.

On a beautiful, sunny afternoon in December 2011, I got my wish. Nine of the girls who were making enough progress to be granted an "outing" were escorted to my home on the outskirts of Atlanta. Jessica was one of them.

My husband and I aren't wealthy by any means, but having a large family means living in a large house, and we are fortunate to have some acreage as well. I'd done it up big-time—with Christmas lights glittering on the branches outside, fresh greenery, and a Christmas tree adorned with crystal lights and family ornaments. I'll never forget Jessica's first words when she walked up the steps and took in the scene: "Ooh, Miss Sandy, you got it goin' on!"

But out of all the Christmas decorations, the girls were most interested in a large basket filled with wrapped presents. One of the girls accidentally bumped the basket, knocking a present onto the floor and revealing one of the name tags I'd tried to hide. Soon a group of them were giggling and pointing at the basket.

"Miss Sandy," one girl ventured, "that present over there has a tag on it that says 'Morisha.' Is that . . . is that for me?"

I assured her that it was and was rewarded with a huge smile.

After warming up in the house, the girls decided to walk through the fields behind our house where my husband was working on his tractor. When they found Douglas, he greeted them and rubbed his shaved head. "If I'd known I was going to meet some ladies today, I would have fixed my hair," he joked.

Those girls came back giggling and talking about what my husband had said. I must have heard them retell the story ten times that afternoon. They couldn't get over the fact that he'd called them "ladies." They had lived with such shame for so long that a simple comment signaling respect was a new and exciting experience.

A Little House and a Husband Who Loves Me

My home includes an upstairs picture window that overlooks the trees on our back property. It offers a beautiful view, especially in the snow. When Jessica saw it, she sat right down in the glider rocking chair at the window and admired the scene.

"Miss Sandy," she broke the silence, "if this was my house, then this would be my chair and nobody but me would sit in it. I would sit here every day and look out at these trees."

"Well, let me tell you girls something," I said. As the girls gathered around me, I realized that some of them probably saw the life I had now and figured I'd had an easy time getting here. I certainly hadn't been through all the horrible experiences they'd endured, but I'd had my share of struggles too. I decided to give them the short version of my life.

I married right out of high school, and after two children and seven very bad years, we divorced. As soon as my divorce was finalized, my church friends abandoned me. I became angry at God. After struggling for three years to make ends meet between two part-time jobs and limited child support, I became even angrier. Rather than trust God to help me, I decided I couldn't trust anyone other than myself. *I* had to fix the situation, even if it meant spreading myself thin to the point of breaking.

So fix it I did. I ran away to Las Vegas with a man who treated me better, who I thought would make a great father to my two children. I had four more wonderful children with him. From the outside, it looked like we were living the good life, growing a family, making good money—but on the inside I was tormented.

After moving eighteen times in twelve years, we too divorced. I was a backup singer for various music artists including the award-winning gospel singer Andraé Crouch, but the overwhelming stress I felt soon stole my voice, and my career with it. I filed for bankruptcy. I realized too late that by "fixing" my situation, I had only made matters worse for myself, and most importantly, for my children.

The girls just sat and listened. I had never seen them so quiet.

One day, I told them, I was driving to one of my two jobs, watching the trees along the side of the road rush by, when the despair overtook me. I pulled over, the tears falling from my face. "Lord," I said, "if You would just give me a house, just a little house with some trees, and a husband who loves me and is loyal to me, I don't think I'd ever ask You for anything else again."

The Lord heard that prayer. He blessed me with a wonderful husband and a home beyond my asking. I told the girls that my husband had struggled with a range of addictions, and the baggage we both brought to our marriage came at a cost. I told them we had made the decision six years ago to become serious Christ-followers, to forgive those who had hurt us, to live a life pleasing to God, and to depend upon Him for healing our hurts. I told them I wished I had learned earlier in life what I now knew—that choosing to follow Christ without hesitation brings happiness and healing in ways I never expected. Today, we enjoy the wonderful marriage God intended.

"Even when you don't think God is anywhere around," I said, "when you don't acknowledge His presence, or when you're doing everything wrong, He is there and He hears you. He will answer your prayers."

That day at my house was a turning point for Jessica, and I hope for others as well. After saying my goodbyes to my guests headed back to Wellspring, I watched Jessica walk slowly through the living room and down the outside front steps. Suddenly she stopped, turned around, and stood in the doorway. "I just want one more look," she said.

Jessica seemed lost in thought as she took in the Christmas scene our house held before her. She gave me just a hint of a smile.

> "Ever since I went to Miss Sandy's house, and sat in her chair and heard her story, I realized that even when I don't know God, He knows me."

I wondered what she was thinking so hard about. I wondered if she was thinking a house and home like this could one day be hers. God was dealing with her heart.

About a week later, one of Jessica's therapists called, her voice rising in excitement. "Jessica has had *such* a major turnaround," she said. "When we asked her what was going on, she said, 'Ever since I went to Miss Sandy's house, and sat in her chair and looked out her window and heard her story, I realized that even when I don't know God, He knows me. He hears me, and He knows what I want and what I need. He sees my heart. I'm determined that my life is going to be different. The end is not going to be like the beginning.'"

Providing a Picture of God

Looking out at the trees from our upstairs window, Jessica got a glimpse of what her life could be. I think it expanded her vision for her life beyond the pain of her past, giving her hope for the future. When these girls realize that you've weathered storms of your own and that God made something beautiful through it, a light clicks on in their heads. If you can accept them for who they are despite what they've done, just like God accepts you in spite of what you've done, it gives them a picture of who God is, and a picture of what their life could look like through His transformative grace. To me, that is the heart of Wellspring.

I continue to try to paint this picture for the girls in my current position as Wellspring's project manager of new transitional housing. This service is for girls who are nearing the end of the program and getting ready to graduate into independent life. We work very hard to create a beautiful place for them to live, a home that includes beds, sheets, comforters, and artwork on the walls. I love to watch the girls take it in for the first time. It's an environment that is lovely, peaceful, and safe—a sharp contrast to their former surroundings where they lived as prisoners in the world of sex trafficking.

It Could Have Been Me

One of the reasons I first decided to get involved with Wellspring is very personal.

When I was in my early twenties, I worked for a large clothing manufacturer as a model of the clothing lines we offered to prospective buyers. One day, the president of the company offered me a huge promotion if I would take my job outside the office. He told me I could make even more money if I decided to have sex with the clothing buyers. I turned his offer down. But as a struggling single mom, I did briefly consider it. *Maybe,* I thought, *by the time my precious son is old enough to know how I made our living, I could switch to a legitimate job like secretary work, and no one will ever know.* But God stepped in and prevented me from making that catastrophic mistake. I realize now what a disaster that would have been for me and my children—and how easy it is for anyone to be lured into the sex trade. When I read the statistics about human trafficking, I remember that it could have been me.

I believe we are called to make a difference, to stand up for those who can't defend themselves. I know that if I had ventured down that dark road as a single mom, I would have wanted someone to stand up for me.

We don't have to give a million dollars or build a big organization to fight a cause. I try to teach my kids that we can all do something kind for others every day—whether it's giving a pair of shoes to someone in need or simply offering a compliment. There are countless opportunities—such as reading to a child, mentoring a teen, or even teaching sex trafficking survivors how to cook.

These things do not require much on our part, and mean everything to those who need help. If everyone will just do *something*, we will change the world.

04~ My Story

My heart for the helpless was first sparked into
action because of my brother.

I was in first grade in the small town of Geneva,
Alabama, skipping rope on the playground, when I
heard the taunts. A third-grader was yelling at one of
his classmates—my brother—saying that Robert was "dumb." I'd
heard the cruel remarks before. Robert had Down syndrome and was
often the victim of thoughtless teasing.

I didn't move. The bully was, after all, much taller than me. But
then he made a mistake. He pushed Robert, not once, but twice.
Suddenly I was too mad to care about how big that bully was. I
stomped over there and gave him a bloody nose.

Maybe I've always had a heart for the underdog, for the people who
are pushed around by the bullies in this world. Yet I've never thought
of myself as any kind of savior. For a long time, in fact, my dream was
to be a mom and kindergarten teacher, to raise a family, shape the
lives of little children for twenty years, and then retire.

My plan was off to a good start when I married my high school
sweetheart. For the next nine years, I enjoyed a blissful life. When my
first child, a son, was born, I couldn't have been happier.

But then my bliss turned into my worst nightmare. What I thought
was a perfect marriage ended abruptly. Almost overnight, everything

had changed, and I felt alone and abandoned—far from the dream for my life I had wanted. Suddenly I knew what it felt like to be betrayed by someone you love. Suddenly *I* was the underdog, fighting to find a shred of hope so I could make it through another day. Only the compassion of a few caring friends—along with the love of my great God—allowed me to endure that terrible time.

A few years later, God brought an amazing man into my life. Dick and I married, became active in our church, had a son together, and enjoyed raising our family in Peachtree City, Georgia. But the Lord had a plan that would again shake up my world.

The Beginning of Wellspring Living

In 1993 I met Sara, the hairdresser with desperate family circumstances. I felt strangely stirred to do what I could to help her, even if I didn't know exactly how. At the same time, I began serving as women's ministry director at my church. Then, in 1999, a friend asked if I would cochair a two-day event titled "Just Give Me Jesus," a gathering designed to bring different cultures and believers together in Atlanta to strengthen disciples and the church. The obvious candidates for directing the conference had turned the opportunity down, so I became the improbable choice charged with organizing an event attended by twenty thousand women.

As our wonderful planning team came together, something incredible happened. We prayed together, formed friendships, and this massive undertaking turned into a successful event because a great group of women decided to stand together. Once it was over, however, we weren't ready to stop. We had just spent a weekend learning of a multitude of needs in our city. We decided to continue meeting and praying for hurting people in Atlanta.

Our prayers and conversations coalesced into an idea—*we* could take action and make a difference. Soon we had a team of forty ordinary women praying and envisioning a new reality for our city and beyond, a vision that launched Wellspring Living, named after the living water that Jesus promised the Samaritan woman at the well. From the start, our goal was to seek God for the suffering young women of our city, to bridge the gap between the church and those who were in the midst of despair yet uncomfortable in a church setting. But how? We really didn't know what we were getting ourselves into. We just saw a great need, so we opened up a home to women in desperate circumstances who were referred to us by partnering organizations in the city.

We were kindergarten teachers, housewives, and community advocates, praying and seeking God's direction as to how we could best channel our joint passion and service. What kind of program was needed to help desperate souls in Atlanta?

Later, when a conference speaker challenged us to look at our Wellspring Living clients and find the common link in their life stories, we realized the common thread among the girls we hoped to serve was childhood sexual abuse.

> At the time, the subject of abuse was virtually ignored inside the walls of the church. Yet one in four girls is abused sexually before age eighteen.

At the time, the subject of abuse was virtually ignored inside the walls of the church. Yet according to the Centers for Disease Control and Prevention, one in four girls is abused sexually before she reaches the age of eighteen.[7] This statistic is so alarming that we could not ignore the truth we'd discovered, even if it was difficult to broach with the faith community.

The damage from just one incident is life-altering. Emotionally, girls are arrested in their development and make choices based on their emotional age at the time of the abuse. No wonder they make so many destructive decisions! Mentally, there are so many breakdowns in the brain that a learning disability is often the result. Socially, the concept of a healthy relationship becomes distorted and dysfunctional. Spiritually, the girls become disconnected from the Lord. How can a girl learn to trust a God who seems unable to protect her when someone she should be able to trust—a family member or friend—fails to protect her?

What a complicated situation! To educate us to address this situation, God brought us experts, resources, and licensed counselors to work with the girls and their trauma and abuse. He led us to read and study everything we could get our hands on about recovery and tangible methods that would strengthen our interactions with the girls. We also had to learn how to develop a program that would not be overwhelming for the girls or for us. *Seven Practices of Effective Ministry* by Andy Stanley, Lane Jones, and Reggie Joiner, was a pivotal resource as we nailed down clear objectives (wins) and methods (steps) for our program.[8] We decided that the goal we would aim for with every girl we served would be a restored life, as we would empower her to make strong steps toward wholeness in her body, soul, and spirit.

Growing a Program

As a kindergarten teacher from a family full of boys and with no social services experience, even I had to wonder why I was appointed by our group to be the director of a center for girls. But I believe this decision is reflective of 1 Corinthians 1:27, "But God chose the foolish things of the world to shame the wise; God chose the weak things of the world to shame the strong." It was my very deficiency that required me to rely fully on God for His ability to bring in the experts needed to create a program that would do the impossible in the lives of so many hurting girls. So in 2001, with high hopes, we incorporated Wellspring Living—a completely subsidized residential program in a therapeutic environment for young women who had suffered from childhood sexual abuse.

I still remember our first client. Danielle was twenty-four. As a little girl, she'd been physically, verbally, and sexually abused. As an adult, she tried to forget her past through drinking, drugs, prostitution, and encounters with the occult. Five months before coming to us, when none of these distractions worked anymore, Danielle had tried to take her own life.

We stood in front of the Atlanta condominium where she would live with Laura, our first staff member who would serve as a house parent and Danielle's new "coach." Danielle wore tennis shoes and overalls, both full of holes. Strands of greasy, dishwater-blonde hair stuck out from under a tattered denim hat. Her shoulders sagged. Her head was down. She looked like a leafless twig that would snap at the first hint of a strong breeze.

I didn't have a clue what to say.

"Danielle," I stammered, "it's so good to see you." I cautiously put my arm around her back for a hug. She gave me a limp-armed hug in return. Then I saw tears on her face. Whether she was excited, nervous, relieved, or scared, I didn't know.

There were many unknowns in this tenuous beginning, for both of us.

The first few years of Wellspring Living involved constant refinement and learning. At pivotal points along the way, the right people and resources came to us, helping us understand the core values God wanted us to have in place. A comprehensive approach was primary.

The program would look at the needs of the whole person and aim to move her toward a healthy lifestyle, not just away from addictive drugs or other poor choices that are often the result in the lives of the abused. She needed to become a wise and connected person in her relationships, rectify broken relationships, and set healthy boundaries. Finally, convinced that God is the healer, we desired to see our girls develop an intimate relationship with the Lord and with a community of faith. More than anything, this is what would support each girl for the rest of her life.

The journey into wholeness is unique for each person, so we needed to create a system that would allow us to serve girls using high-quality individualized care. Creating a plan of care involved assessing each individual's needs. As we prayed about this, our team found a model for care in Deuteronomy 6. In this passage, God tells Moses how to help the next generation to know and trust Him. God instructs Moses to tell the children of Israel about Him when they arise in the morning, when they sit down throughout the day, when they walk along the path, and when they lie down at night. In other words, God wanted His people to teach His ways not just in clearly defined teachable moments, but also in the grit of day-to-day life.

> We had to become vulnerable enough to get into the mud of their "stuff," to listen to them, cry with them, and wait for them.

We knew an organized program was necessary for recovery, but this verse also showed us that we needed to go beyond the program itself. We realized that the core where life transformation happens is in the day to day, which is not always confined to curriculum and classes. So we decided at Wellspring Living we would do both. We would have both direct care workers, such as counselors and teachers, as well as shift workers, who would be with the girls throughout the day in ordinary activities such as meals and downtime. This unique structure would support both individual counseling sessions for the girls and also the opportunity for them to live with trusted mentors who would be available to them at any time, for any need.

Building a model that supports this comprehensive process required connections with many volunteers and partners. Collaboration was another essential core value that enriched the work God had called us to do and kept us from seeing ourselves as the single source in a girl's recovery.

We each had to learn to become vulnerable enough to get into the mud and mire of their "stuff," to listen to them, cry with them, and wait for them. As we walk with them, we must believe the best for them. One thing I love about our coaches is that if you walked through the Wellspring home, you couldn't tell the difference between a coach and a client. Our coaches don't speak down to the girls. They speak to them at equal level, eye to eye.

Finally, we determined flexibility was a necessary core value so that the organization could adjust when God spoke. Being adaptable was important not only for dealing with the girls but also for the overall strategic ministry plan. It wasn't always easy, and often made us feel uncomfortable, but a willingness to stay agile so we could move when God was orchestrating refinement was essential.

Today, the hard work that so many have invested in Wellspring is evident in the smiles and success stories of our graduates (www.the whiteumbrellacampaign.com/video/#Graduate). We have four programs:

- Wellspring Living Women's Program: a residential recovery home for adult survivors of childhood sexual abuse

- Lynn Sweet Counseling Center: a care center that provides therapeutic outpatient services for the greater surrounding community
- Wellspring Redeemed Assessment Center: a safe place for women escaping unsafe situations while considering long-term recovery
- Wellspring Living Girls' Program: a therapeutic and educational program for child survivors of forced prostitution and sex trafficking

Thanks to a donor base of nearly five thousand people who give time, money, and other resources, Wellspring now serves one hundred women and girls annually. Nearly four hundred have graduated from our programs, starting with Danielle, the girl who came to us unkempt and uncertain. Danielle flourished in the program, became our first successful graduate, and married three years after joining us. Like her, the majority of young women in the Wellspring programs have successfully left their past behind and stepped into a brighter and more fulfilling future.

A New Challenge: Wellspring for Girls

In February of 2007, our facility was filled with women and some girls in our recovery program for childhood sexual abuse. I thought we were living out God's vision for Wellspring Living Girls' Program—but then He showed me there was more work to be done in our city. Atlanta Mayor Shirley Franklin was speaking at a breakfast downtown, and someone introduced us, mentioning that Wellspring worked with women who were survivors of childhood sexual abuse. Then Mayor Franklin looked me in the eyes and said, "Mary Frances, we need you to get involved in the sex trafficking of our children of Atlanta."

Well, I certainly didn't anticipate such a challenge. We had just completed a new, larger facility for our adult program participants.

I thought we were on the right track and didn't feel ready to take on a new project, especially at this level. I told the mayor that I would research the issue and be available to consult with anyone who wanted to engage it.

I researched what was happening to girls in Atlanta, and I was appalled at what I found—395 underage girls were being exploited monthly. They were expected to earn $1,000 per night for their pimps, meaning they would be violated eight to ten times each evening. The average age of the girls lured into the Atlanta sex trade is twelve. The further I delved into this issue, the sicker I became to think that these young girls were experiencing crisis on a daily basis, as regularly as other twelve-year-olds do their homework.

Yet I didn't think Wellspring Living had the resources, financially and otherwise, to get involved. Later in the fall, another kind encourager challenged me saying, "I believe Wellspring Living must be involved in this issue." My response was the same: our financial obligations will not allow us to do that, but we are happy to consult.

About two weeks later, a group reached out to me, asking me to advise them on how to open a facility for girls. The night before our first meeting, I was home alone, getting ready for bed, when I looked at the ceiling in my family room and prayed a simple prayer: "God, I really don't know if what we've been doing for the past seven years would work with girls who have been trafficked. I really don't know what to say to these women tomorrow. So, if You have any ideas, would You please send them my way?"

Then I went to bed and slept soundly. As I read Scripture the next morning, a memory of a conversation I'd had three years earlier flew through my head. At that time, we at Wellspring were looking for a way to expand our services, and I was speaking with a representative of a local organization that owned some unused residential property.

Nothing resulted from that conversation, but one sentence came into my mind that stopped my thoughts this morning—"We always have an empty children's cottage."

"God," I cried out, "is this *You*? Is this a possibility?"

After all, if someone didn't have to get a children's home license and a facility, a program could be developed relatively quickly to address this urgent need. I pulled out my computer and began to write down every possibility. At a Starbucks on a rainy fall Tuesday afternoon, I presented this plan to the group of women who wanted to open a children's facility. I was sure this was God's solution to the problem and that these women would take my suggestions and get something up and running soon.

Two months later, however, nothing had happened.

At Wellspring's board retreat in November, I presented a new option to our members. "Do you want me to go through a discovery process," I asked, "to see if God wants us to begin a program for survivors of sex trafficking?" Unanimously, they said yes. The adventure began with a search for an empty children's facility. I first left a message for the representative I'd recalled speaking with. To this day, he has yet to return my phone call. I then turned to two other organizations. These officials each had empty facilities but felt it wouldn't be something they wanted to undertake. Maybe their work was too demanding at the time. Maybe they were afraid of the kind of people we were talking about.

On a cool afternoon in February 2008, I was down to my last option. I decided to meet with a representative of a licensed child-care agency. I remember praying on the way to the meeting, "Lord, I thought this was Your plan, but it's been rejected everywhere I've turned. So if this is Your plan, You are going to have to make this happen. I can't convince anyone to do this!"

To my surprise, this representative wanted to form a partnership. "I'm willing to take a risk," he said, "for a new program that would serve children." They had a "cottage" available that would be just what we needed.

On my drive home, I could hardly contain my excitement and gratitude. "Lord, I didn't think anyone was going to step up and do this," I prayed. "We had the dream, yet I didn't see reality connecting to it. But You knew! As always, Your timing is just right. Thank You, thank You!"

Less than a month later, I met with then Georgia Governor Sonny Perdue to tell him what God had placed on our hearts for young girls who were victims of sex trafficking. We talked more than thirty minutes. Toward the end of the conversation, the governor asked me to meet with his wife, Mary, as well as with the commissioner of juvenile justice, the state child advocate, and the executive director of

> God pushed this issue to the forefront of the state even though I knew no one and had no political influence.

the Governor's Office for Children and Families. God had just pushed this issue to the forefront of the state of Georgia even though I knew no one and had no political influence. And soon all the vital children's agencies came together! In October 2008, we accepted our first client into the Wellspring Living Girls' Program.

Today, Wellspring Living Girls' Program has the capacity to serve up to sixteen young women at any given time. We offer a holistic approach: counseling, group therapy, education, life skills and vocational training, family reunification, and spiritual care. We collaborate with a licensed children's home, a nontraditional school, and individuals and groups in the community to promote healing, practical help, and most important of all, hope.

We are still on a journey of growth and development, but one thing has become very clear to me: God cares deeply about oppressed and victimized children, the true underdogs in our world. He will move in amazing ways to accomplish His purposes to rescue and restore these precious young women. To play a part in what He is doing is a wonderful privilege, one that keeps me humbled and in awe of Him every day.

05~ Her Battle

Lindsay Bowley, a middle school teacher
in Atlanta and my daughter-in-law, has
always been interested in what motivates
her students to behave the way they
do. When she began learning about sex
trafficking, she was astonished at what
the research showed.

by Lindsay Bowley

One out of every four. I have repeated this statistic over and over
and still cannot fathom the depth of what it really means. One out
of every four girls is sexually abused before the age of eighteen. For
boys, the number is one out of six.[9] This means one out of every four
women at the grocery store, at the bank, at the mall, in the pew at
church, and everywhere in "normal" life have had this traumatic experience. For me as a teacher, this means that one out of every four of
my precious eighth grade girls will, before they graduate from high
school, become one of those victims.

And these are only the reported cases. The numbers, staggering as
they are, are probably higher than we think. As a teacher and a care-
taker of children, I must understand what happens to a minor who
has been abused in such a way. Actually, we all need to shoulder this
responsibility. As members of society, we need to be clued in to what

makes sexual abuse victims behave the way they do.

Unfortunately, labeling is an easy, one-size-fits-all remedy that helps us (including myself) deal with those we cannot understand. But this Band-Aid solution serves only to further harm the walking wounded, people we come in contact with every day. Taking the time to understand how God created the brain to work and the body to react to trauma can help us better respond to those among us who are hurting, wounded, and broken.

Most abuse victims are not easy to spot, and there is no stereotype for a sexual abuse victim. She does not necessarily have to come from a single-parent household with a low socioeconomic status. Her ethnicity does not make her trauma more likely, nor does the city where she lives. Instead, she could be a work associate, a child in Sunday school, or a kid at the neighborhood bus stop. Well-meaning people often act upon misguided assumptions about who is abused, yet so many of these hurting children are slipping right under their good-natured noses. The reality is that there is no profile for these silent sufferers.

Because there is no stereotypical victim, it is important to learn to pay attention to the signs of sexual abuse. We do know the majority of sexual abuse happens between the vulnerable ages of seven and thirteen. The average age that abuse begins is at age eight. Shockingly, many cases of infant sexual abuse have also been reported.[10] This is not easy to think about. When the truth comes out that a teenage girl was sexually abused, she was likely the victim of this horrendous act years before it was noticed. Without knowing it, many caretakers, such as parents, teachers, mentors, or anyone else in a position of influence in a child's life, are completely unaware of the warning signs. They brush off serious repercussions resulting from childhood trauma simply as "bad behavior."[11]

It's easy to miss the signs. I understood this better after I met Alisha. Alisha is a beautiful young woman, only a few years younger than me, who loves and creates beautiful art and music. We laughed together as we sat at a local coffee shop. Never in my life would I have profiled her as someone who had been trafficked, yet Alisha was pushed into the sex trade by one of her own family members.

As I heard more of her story I began to realize that on the outside, she lived a normal life, but on the inside, her self-worth had slowly decayed into a hollow cavity. For years, she blended in at school and even in church, as her pain passed undetected and unnoticed. She told me that when anyone ever did see something strange in the way she viewed the world, they would respond with the Christian cliché, "You just need to get closer to God." For years, not a single friend, mentor, or confidante was able to read the signs nor realize that the abuse that began at such a young age had warped Alisha's understanding of what is normal. But the survivor's inaccurate perception of what is normal has more to do with patterns in the brain than a question of faith.

Abuse and the Developing Brain

In fact, the younger the child at the onset of sexual abuse, the more devastating and lasting the impact of that abuse will be on the victim's perception. Research has shown that a child's brain is extremely malleable.[12] Like clay, it can be molded and shaped by the guiding hands of experience. When a baby is born, his or her brain is not fully formed.

This unique and fascinating organ grows from bottom to top. The first part of the brain to develop is the section that regulates various essential systems in the body such as breathing or signaling the heart to beat. The ability to think abstractly or understand relationships develops much later in childhood. Like a series of building blocks, each portion of the brain that develops provides a foundation for further development, so the brain's higher functioning abilities depend entirely on those early, basic "building blocks" of development. What this means is that a traumatic event can interrupt the brain's development at any time, and shake it so powerfully that it changes the way the rest of the brain continues to grow. This trauma literally provides the foundation for a child's further understanding of the world.[13]

If sexual abuse occurs at age four, for example, everything that develops in the mind after that point will be influenced by the brain's reaction to that traumatic experience. Blocks that are placed on top of an unstable foundation will cause the whole structure to be unbalanced and unstable. Any pressure applied to such an unstable foundation may cause the entire structure to topple.

Environmental cues can also change the course in the developing brain by redefining what is considered "normal." Experiences provide templates in the brain that determine how life is interpreted, as well as what makes a person laugh, cry, love, hate, remember events, and create beliefs. It also controls what each person views as "safe." These environmental cues teach children what they can trust and what they should fear.

Because the brain is so formative and vulnerable in these early years, childhood abuse influences how a person makes decisions and assesses risk later in life. Unfortunately, abuse is often inflicted by someone close to a child, such as a parent or relative. Frequently, it is repetitive. The red flags warning of a dangerous situation are often missed by victims of abuse because their framework of understanding is completely altered. The way they view risk and very real danger is clouded by their prior experiences. When a dangerous situation presents itself, the victim's brain doesn't send warning messages the way a healthy brain ordinarily would.[14]

I observed this during a conversation with one of my middle school students last year. This fourteen-year-old told me how sad she was that her boyfriend, also fourteen, was in jail for the second time. He had fathered a child with another girl and struggled with drug abuse, on top of major anger issues. Under the influence of her love-tinted glasses, this young woman was willing to forgive and walk back into a dangerous situation. I learned later in our conversation that she had been sexually abused at age three. Her judgment was not as it should have been. A traumatic event that happened eleven years earlier created a distorted framework for how she would recognize and analyze risk.

The Reset Button: Trauma and the Brain's Response

Normal everyday tasks involve only specific portions of the brain. For example, one area of the brain is used when learning new material while another area is accessed during an activity that involves repetitive use of motor skills. But when abuse happens, every part of the brain is accessed all at once because it is responding to a threat. In a sense, the brain goes into overdrive. And because this vital organ is still organizing and developing in younger years, this trauma impacts the child more than it would if he or she were older.[15]

God designed the human body to always work to return to a normal state known as *homeostasis*. When trauma occurs, depending on its severity and frequency, serious damage can be done to all parts of the brain, which in turn has lasting consequences for the person's ability to function and process information in all aspects of life. Sadly, when abuse becomes a part of life and is repeated for many years, the victim lives in a perpetual state of fear. The body no longer knows how to get back to the homeostatic state of calmness and peace. The body's concept of "normal" can actually be a state of hypervigilance, where anything could potentially be perceived as a threat. Even when they are not facing an identifiable threat, these victims live in a state of constant fear and anxiety because it is the only way the body has been conditioned to function.[16]

The brain's response to a severe event like sexual abuse can be compared to a reset button, causing all future experiences to be processed and interpreted based on a new template of what is normal. God perfectly designed the human brain this way, to help a person adapt after a traumatic event whenever they are in the face of danger. As a protective mechanism, the brain automatically begins associating anything related to that particular danger as a red flag that shouts a warning, "Go no further!" These red flags occur exponentially more for a victim of abuse than many people understand, but not necessarily in a way that is beneficial to them.

For a woman who has suffered such a traumatic event, the mere sight of a person who reminds her of her perpetrator, a tone of voice, or a seemingly unsafe situation that brings up distressing memories can cause this person to go into a state of alarm. She becomes re-traumatized, and her entire brain prepares to respond to the threat. Generalized reminders can trigger these responses, and because the victim of abuse is in a constant state of sensitivity to these threats, she can jump from vague apprehension to a state of crippling fear within seconds. Therefore, a sexually abused teenage girl may assess risk like a child and respond to harmless actions of authority as if that person intends to do her harm.

This reaction is often seen when someone from the military returns from a tour of duty—in a condition known as post-traumatic stress disorder, or PTSD. Ordinary sights and sounds that never seemed threatening before can trigger a fight-or-flight response. A friend of mine told me that when her husband came home from serving overseas in the Middle East, he jumped into a state of alarm any time he saw a plastic bag on the side of the road. Most people wouldn't view this as a sign of danger, but her husband associated the piece of trash with a roadside bomb from his tour of duty. This same sense of hypervigilance is often found in victims of sexual abuse. Statistically speaking, we interact on a daily basis with sex abuse victims (whether we know it or not) who are in a perpetual state of sensitivity to potential danger, who are living in a state of unrecognized or unacknowledged fear.

Two Responses to Threats

When fear sets in, people generally respond in one of two ways. Although responses are not necessarily gender-specific, generally boys respond by fighting or fleeing, and girls respond by dissociating.

In a fight-or-flight reaction, a person in the face of danger experiences a rush of adrenaline as the body prepares itself for a physical response. That response can be manifested in several ways. When a person fights, the body goes kicking and screaming in full force to resist against danger. When a person flees, the body undergoes the same physical preparation in order to run as far away from danger as possible.[17]

Abuse victims who have experienced trauma provoking the fight-or-flight response typically develop disorders related to being in this continuous state of hyperarousal. These disorders manifest themselves externally, revealing themselves in the forms of ADHD, hyperactivity, noncompliance, and extreme defiance. Caretakers are often able to spot boys with abuse in their histories easier than girls because these external disorders often cause boys to clash with authority figures. The ratio of boys getting help at an early age for these issues as compared to girls is 3 to 1.[18]

When trauma happens repeatedly as opposed to an isolated event, the fight-or-flight response can progress into a dissociative response. Girls are more likely to initially exhibit this response than boys.[19] The dissociative response occurs when the abuse victim tries to "go to another place" in her mind in order to disengage from what is happening to her. There are many techniques of dissociating. Some children live in a fantasy world created in their head. Some begin daydreaming. Others take on a completely different persona. Many report feeling as if they are floating or watching a movie. Like a deer caught by a car's headlights, children who are terrorized in abusive situations will actually freeze and become numb, compliant, and unwilling to fight.

It is important to remember that trauma response can be triggered by anything an abuse victim associates with her abuse, and what we may perceive as harmless, she might perceive as a generalized threat. Just a simple reminder of a past abusive incident can hurl a young girl down the destructive cycle of completely disconnecting and disengaging from what is going on around her.[20] This strange behavior is often misunderstood by caretakers, who observe only the surface problems of bad attitude or defiant behavior instead of the deeper cause underneath. Sadly, girls who have been abused often do not show outward signs of what is going on psychologically until they begin exhibiting self-soothing behaviors such as cutting themselves or turning to drug abuse. [21]

Other disorders can develop in male and female victims of abuse alike, such as post-traumatic stress disorder, eating disorders, depression, anxiety, and substance abuse. There is a direct correlation between the severity of childhood sexual abuse and the development of psychological disorders. One disorder that researchers believe may be linked to abuse is schizophrenia. In a recent study, 60 percent of female inpatients diagnosed with this disorder were also victims of childhood sexual abuse. Women who have experienced this type of trauma are more likely than others to experience paranoia, hallucinate, or even hear voices in their head. Many of the women who hear voices actually hear the voice of their perpetrator. The younger the child when abuse begins, the higher the likelihood that she will develop symptoms of schizophrenia that will exist later in adulthood. If these internal schizophrenic symptoms are coupled with drug abuse, imagine how devastating the impact can be on that woman's perception of what is reality and truth.[22]

Where Have We Missed It?

Often good-intended, loving caretakers greatly miss the mark in how they deal with girls who have been abused. If one in four young women the age of eighteen have been abused at some point in their life, we can best respond to them by rejecting the misconceptions surrounding abuse.

Remember, *abuse is not always a choice*. Girls who are survivors of sex trafficking are branded on the streets as prostitutes, sometimes quite literally as their pimp burns his mark on their neck or ankles. But they did not choose this work, and it is doubly tragic when these young women are branded once again by stigma and shame when they walk into the wider community, and even the church.

Many believers do not want to help these young women because they believe that these girls have simply "made a bad choice" and are "getting what they deserve." Many are forced into sex trafficking, and other abuse victims make childish judgment calls with seemingly no appropriate assessment of risk. It is hard for many Christians to understand what is going on in the victim's brain. If a little girl was abused at age eight, she will assess risk as an eight-year-old because her brain has developed templates that allow her abuse to completely form how she views the world. These are not wayward girls who are choosing to rebel. They are young women who have not received help and healing.

Second, *abuse victims believe many untruths.* Because of the way the mind works, many abuse victims do not understand that what is happening to them is bad. They have dissociated so deeply from the traumatizing event that they begin to believe lies. This is why a prostitute who is repeatedly sold and abused by her pimp will still believe that he is actually her boyfriend. Similarly, a sexually abusive father will feed his child lies in order to excuse his own behavior. Imagine what it would be like to be a young child and told by an authority figure "it's not bad." Even worse, imagine telling someone about the abuse and not being believed. This is a common occurrence among abuse victims, and it is understandable how the lines between truth and untruth can be easily blurred. Instead of slapping a "bad kid" label on these girls, the Christian community needs to stand beside them and walk with them through the healing process. Fight the lies of the enemy with truth!

Third, *abuse victims can be retraumatized.* When children are abused, threats become generalized. Even what has the appearance of safety can cause a victim of abuse to be instantly on edge.[23] Caretakers who are not sensitive to this characteristic can immediately, without realizing it, create a wall between themselves and the abuse victim. Tone of voice, body posture, and choice of words can be enough to mentally put that child right back in the middle of a past abusive situation. Sometimes, by allowing her mind to wander, a child can even be retraumatized if she thinks back closely on what happened in the past.

Fourth, *children are* not *resilient*. It is widely believed that children are able to quickly "bounce back" after a harrowing experience; however, this is not the case. Since many children who have been abused don't initially show many signs that the abuse is affecting them, adults often misinterpret this.[24] Some children may even be able to easily talk about the event. Yet in reality, kids are extremely sensitive to trauma because it is internalized. The trauma may not show itself obviously and outwardly, but this experience will profoundly shape their outlook, as experience provides the organizational structure for how a child views everything around them.

Finally, *stable is not always stable.* Many children who are pulled out of abusive situations and placed in the care of loving families do not adjust well. The reason for this is that their brains are conditioned to a state of "normal" that functions best in the terrible situation that they have just been rescued from. Changing the mindset and behavior of an abuse victim cannot happen by simply changing the environment they are in, something that even the most loving caretakers may not understand. Often, creating a new and healthy "normal" for an abused child involves much counseling and work to alter his or her templates of understanding.

The church can make a difference—and indeed, has a responsibility to make a difference—for these hurting girls, boys, women, and men. Jesus Christ came to set the captives free, and Christians have the amazing and humbling opportunity to be His hands and feet in this redemptive rescue. Christ calls us to reach out not only to those who are in physical captivity in brothels and bad situations, but also to those who are captives in their own minds to lies and distorted understanding that was formed by terrible experiences in their past.

It is not easy to work with a victim of abuse because she will often react in ways that seem foreign and obstinate. Nevertheless, much like the four men in the Bible who dug through the roof to get their paralyzed friend to Jesus, we must do whatever it takes to help victims of abuse through the journey of healing. Despite the fear and anxiety that paralyzes them, we must be willing to dig through the muck of false beliefs to bring them to the Truth. Jesus Christ is in the business of bringing freedom for those in bondage. May we as a Christian community reach out to victims with a spirit of compassion and understanding, knowing that there is hope of finding true and lasting healing.

06~ She Heals at Her Own Pace

Dion Stokes is the lead therapist for the Wellspring Living Girls' Program and has worked with numerous girls as they have navigated the ups and downs of the healing process. Dion's explanation of an individual's pace and unique response to therapy and healing brings insight to those serving exploited girls.

by Dion Stokes

The toddler had stretched to his full height, all twenty-eight inches of him. He wobbled a bit, his knees threatening to bend in opposite directions, but he kept a firm grip on the coffee table. He was ten months old and just learning to walk.

The little guy's mother was on her knees just a few feet away. She held out her arms. "C'mon, Michael, you can do it! Just let go and step this way."

Michael raised his brown eyes to his mother's face. His expression seemed to say, "Mom, I'm not too sure about this. It's tougher than it looks!"

When I think about the process of restoration and recovery that our young women journey through, it reminds me of a toddler's first steps. No matter how awful her situation, she operates in the "security" of what she knows. It's difficult to give that up for the unknown. Usually, a toddler is motivated to walk by his parents holding out something he wants: a cracker, a favorite stuffed giraffe, or the open arms that lead to a loving hug. In the same way, a girl trapped in a cycle of exploitation needs someone to be there cheering her on and offering something of value—something better. Whether it's a safe place to lay her head, an opportunity to go to school, or the chance to talk to someone who will listen, she needs a motivating reason to help her let go of the familiar and take those first steps toward healing.

Like a toddler, each one of our girls will stumble. She needs someone there, watching and encouraging her, someone close enough to catch her or pick her up when she falls. She may revert to "crawling" because she doesn't yet have confidence in her ability to walk. As she grows, we need to build up her confidence and help her see the benefits of walking. Most parents have held the hand of their little one while he practices walking, cheering him along at each step, ready to catch him if he falls. Similarly, for our girls the journey into healing isn't a steady run but a race marked by many stops and starts.

The Stages of Change

In order for us to be effective caregivers, mentors, and friends to girls recovering from sexual exploitation, we need patience. We also need an understanding of the psychological progressions they're working through. James Prochaska and Carlo DiClemente developed a model known as Stages of Change,[25] which can be helpful for the caregiver on both of these counts. This model helps us detect when a young woman is ready to change, and it also reminds us that relapse is a natural part of the restoration process. Like a young child just learning how to walk, we need to serve each young woman in recovery according to her readiness to progress. Whether she is crawling, walking, or falling after taking a few steps, our role is to keep standing by her and supporting her at whatever stage she is in. The stages of change include:

- *Precontemplation.* The girl in recovery acknowledges that there are problems in her life but resists the idea of change. For example, she might say, "He's not my perpetrator, he's my boyfriend."
- *Contemplation.* She realizes her need for escape but cannot see a realistic solution.
- *Preparation.* She now recognizes she must make a change and begins planning alternatives to her current lifestyle.
- *Action.* She begins taking steps to address the problem, sometimes on her own, such as getting into school or therapy.
- *Maintenance.* She moves forward in her recovery and starts to feel successful.
- *Relapse.* Something triggers a crisis that causes her to return to her old lifestyle. If she is in an environment that doesn't support her newfound lifestyle, she tends to fall back into old patterns.

Since each girl's unique personality and environment influence her stages of change, some girls move quickly into the maintenance stage and never look back, while others progress slowly through the process and may experience several relapses before getting their feet firmly established.

As we work to support and encourage our girls, it's vital that we are realistic about the challenges they face as they move through these stages. Stephanie and Lauren are two girls who went through our Wellspring program and responded to these stages in two different ways.

Choosing a Family

Stephanie joined Wellspring after being controlled by her pimp, Dre, for over two years. They were originally school friends. Then Dre started hanging with older boys and joined a neighborhood gang. Stephanie began dating Dre. She'd never known her father and rarely saw her mother, who battled a drug addiction. In Dre, Stephanie finally found someone who cared for her. When Dre offered her the chance to be initiated into the gang, she jumped at the chance. They became her family.

But there were conditions to being in this family. After they'd dated a few months, Dre allowed other gang members to rape Stephanie for $200. He told her the gang needed to see if she could be used to generate more income. Soon, Stephanie's photo was posted on websites, and she began walking the streets to bring in money to support the gang.

Stephanie had mixed feelings about her new life. It was often scary, creepy, and exhausting to have sex with men night after night. It also brought up painful memories of childhood abuse that she had long shoved aside. But Dre and the others seemed to appreciate what she did, and this gave her a purpose, a reason for living. They were her family, after all.

But one night took a surprise turn when the man Stephanie was supposed to sleep with turned out to be an undercover policeman. She was arrested for prostitution and held in a juvenile facility. The judge gave her two choices—a recovery program called Wellspring Living or jail.

Stephanie chose Wellspring, but she wasn't happy about it. "I shouldn't be here," she told us. "My friends depend on me. I'm no good to them if I'm locked up."

At first, Stephanie didn't see the point of the program or what we were trying to teach her. Twice during those first few months, she tried to run away. But the second time she ran away, finally back on the street like she wanted, she questioned if this really was the life she wanted. Having spent time at Wellspring Living, she finally had something to compare her old life to, and she wondered who cared about her more—Dre and the gang, or the Wellspring staff. When Stephanie returned safely to us, she began to open her heart and receive the good news of hope and healing we offered. She saw that she had value and that God valued her.

"I know where my real family is," she said. "I want to be part of God's family now."

Stephanie worked through the trauma of her childhood emotional and sexual abuse, her broken relationships, her life with the gang, her self-esteem, and her spiritual connection with God. She was on the journey toward healing and restoration. She went back to school with credits that put her on track for graduation and found a part-time job at a local fast-food restaurant. When Stephanie graduated from the program with all of our best wishes and a plan for continuing contact and support, things were looking up for her.

Five months later, however, Stephanie voluntarily returned to her old life. She ignored our attempts to contact her. Today we continue to pray for Stephanie and ask about her, but we don't know where she is.

Why does this happen? Why is it hard for someone to recognize that a change needs to be made? How can a girl be so successful in turning her life around, accepting change, and working toward a better future, yet return to a life she knows is harmful?

There are so many "whys" and not enough answers. We all do what we can to support and encourage our girls, to give them a spiritual and practical foundation for the future, but in the end, the path they choose is up to them. Stephanie has relapsed, but she may yet come to a point where she wants to try again. If and when she calls, we'll be ready for her.

Stepping into the Light

Lauren also came to Wellspring after being caught up in sexual exploitation by someone she considered a boyfriend. He was everything to her. When she came to us as a result of a court order, Lauren didn't want anyone to help her. She hadn't even considered the very first stage of contemplation. Lauren resisted all of our attempts in therapy to help her see truth. She was convinced that life outside the Wellspring home was better and that she didn't need God or us.

> Ultimately, God brings permanent change. Our task is to hold out our arms as these young women learn to walk again.

Two weeks after entering the program, Lauren and another girl, Dana, ran away from the home. It seemed Lauren's ears were filled with cotton and she hadn't heard anything we'd said, yet what she did next proved otherwise.

Lauren and Dana hid in a grove of pine trees in a woodsy section just beyond the property of the Wellspring home while they waited for Dana's pimp to pick them up. As they waited, Lauren's mind filled with doubts and questions.

I had to get out of there. It was just too weird. Everybody pretends to be nice, but I know it's only a matter of time until that changes. Only . . . what now? This guy picks us up and we go where? Back to walking the streets and barely getting enough to eat and getting high on who knows what?

The thrill of escaping faded as Lauren considered what was next. *Maybe this wasn't such a great idea. Maybe, God—if You are out there, please help me get to where I need to be.*

A few minutes later, a patrol car drove slowly past. The officer noticed movement in the trees, and when he pointed his flashlight at the girls, Lauren felt that God was answering her prayer. Though Dana tried to hold her back, Lauren stepped out of the trees and into the light.

Lauren returned to Wellspring. The Lord's intervention on the night she ran away propelled her into the final maintenance stage of change. She never relapsed. At the time of this writing, Lauren is a senior in high school. She attended her prom last spring and is looking forward to graduation. She plans to go to college and become a social worker who helps other girls just like her.

Change, even good change, is difficult. Each girl responds differently to the opportunity. As her support team, we must be the ever-present voice that cheers her on and coaches her to keep pursuing healthy change. Ultimately, it is God who brings permanent change. Our task is to seek His will even as we hold out our arms to these young women learning to walk again, encouraging them to take one more wobbly step forward.

07~ Peeling Back the Layers

No one is in a better position to describe the complex journey toward a girl's healing than a therapist who has listened to her stories and worked with her through her pain. Mindy Pierce, a therapist at Wellspring Living Women's Program, contributed this chapter so that we can understand how to best stand with that girl.

by Mindy Pierce

A therapist's job is all about time—time spent peeling back layers by listening, asking questions, and listening some more. When a young woman enters the therapeutic portion of her recovery journey at Wellspring, the first several counseling sessions are devoted to gathering a history and attempting to understand her context, background, and the host of complexities that have contributed to her destructive patterns.

Typically, an initial assessment or "psychosocial evaluation" may be completed in a forty-five or sixty-minute session, yet so many of our girls have experienced such complex trauma that gleaning this information from them takes more of a time investment. They've spent years numbing, avoiding, "forgetting," or medicating the painful past.

The waves of abuse, trauma, and lies have taught them that their voice doesn't matter, and that they are responsible for their problems even when they never invited the abuse. Therapy also poses issues because these girls often view trust as merely a gateway for hurt, rejection, or exploitation. They feel that only a fool would believe that someone else might care for their best interest. Thus, we must invest significant time in listening to their stories. They rarely unfold quickly.

One reason for this slow unraveling is that our girls may not realize at first that certain pieces of their history are significant. As we continue to talk, eventually they may think, *Maybe I wasn't crazy after all to be upset about that, even though everybody kept telling me to get over it. Maybe it is worth talking about.*

At Wellspring, we have observed that the most volatile time for a young woman who has been sexually exploited is often just after she leaves that life. She may have spent years protecting herself from the truth—numbing the memories with alcohol, drugs, sex, an eating disorder, or cutting. She may have shut down emotionally and avoided all efforts by others to help. When she finally exits this life of manipulative abuse and gains perspective through distance, she often comes face-to-face with a conclusion that is too horrific to digest. Sadly, the despair of that moment may propel her into more destructive choices rather than into freedom. She may even end her life. It's as if her life story has been scrawled out on paper, then read by someone else, ripped up, and burned before her eyes. Often our well-intentioned but inappropriate message is received as, "That was a horrible life. Now you can start over . . . from scratch!"

As a girl seeking recovery, you are suddenly hit with several devastating realizations all at once. You learn that your former identity is void of true value. You realize that you were never truly loved but only used as a replaceable commodity. And possibly the hardest realization to accept, you now see that you did not engage in exploitation out of free will as you perhaps convinced yourself, but out of desperation, lack of options, manipulation, force, or as a result of deep wounds or unmet hunger for love and acceptance.

When one of our girls faces these truths, it is critical that we recognize the emotional weight of these realizations and respond with patience, grace, and support. If we're not careful, we will say, "God loves you and wants to offer you restoration! Let's start over!" with great conviction and optimism, while she's still registering, "You were never really loved by the people you trusted, and your life has amounted to nothing but utter ruin." What we intend as a positive message may have the reverse effect and overwhelm her.

A person is capable of digesting only so much truth at one time. This is why our therapy sessions start with a history that may be initially vague. I listen for trauma wounds and for the lies she tells about herself, others, and God that she assimilated from those wounds. Then, slowly, we begin confronting the lies and naming experiences accurately.

It Takes Patience

One of the most common lies I hear is the deep sense of personal shame and responsibility a woman may feel from early sexual molestation or what was perhaps mislabeled "mutual" and "consensual" sexual acting out. I hear these words all the time:

"I didn't say no loud or firm enough."

"I didn't resist or fight hard enough."

"I didn't scream."

"I didn't get up and run out of the room as soon as he walked in."

"I never told my mom. If I had, maybe she would have made it stop."

The false beliefs behind these statements make it hard for these girls to see what happened to them as abuse.

To counteract this, together we consider the definition of "true consent" and explore the idea that if she sensed her no would not have been honored by her abuser, then her yes (such as not fighting back) did not equate to being responsible for the sexual attention.

In therapy, this process of self-revelation, identifying lies, speaking truth, and experiencing the Lord's healing slowly builds trust. As counselors, we aim to show no judgment or loathing toward the girl or the offender, yet we do name the offender's action as wrong and hurtful and cite the offender as responsible. We offer a reinterpreted context for her to understand how her pain caused feelings that resulted in a desire to escape those feelings. We help her make sense of her behaviors and articulate her secrets. All of these tasks are a part of hearing her story. This process of listening and drawing her out is a vehicle for building trust; transforming her view of self, the Lord, and others; and helping her experience restoration and new revelations.

> This process of listening and drawing her out is a vehicle for building trust; transforming her view of self, the Lord, and others.

Peeling back one layer and healing it exposes the next. As we go deeper, a girl may say, "You know, I've never told anyone about this because I was too embarrassed [or because it didn't seem important . . . she was afraid . . . she didn't think anyone would believe her . . . or she thought it was her fault]. But I think you should know."

If these traumas are mentioned at all early on in counseling, it's typically in conjunction with, "But that was years ago and I'm over it now." The hidden message behind this tough talk is often, "I have spent a *lot* of energy and time trying to numb myself from feelings and to forget anything associated with this painful event. I would rather not talk about it. I choose to ignore these painful emotions rather than confront them, because I'm fairly certain I wouldn't survive those overwhelming feelings."

When we are patient, however, she will eventually begin to talk about her most deeply buried secrets she is terrified to talk about, believes she's responsible for, and hates herself for.

It Takes an Individual Approach

Through this unhurried process, each girl teaches me a lot about herself. I learn not only facts about her past but also her tendencies in responding to conflicts, her areas of strength and weakness, her personal resources, how she processes things, how much honesty or confrontation she can successfully manage, how she best receives truth, her signals when she's overwhelmed and shutting down, and how I can best reengage with her and approach these hidden land mines with caution.

Shawna had a rare neurological condition that impacted her experience of the world around her, as well as our every interaction. I was concerned that if I asked Shawna too many questions about her abuse, she might believe that I saw her as some kind of circus freak. But I knew I could not comprehend her or her world, or learn how to help her, if I didn't understand this significant part of her life. After reading and taking notes for a few weeks, I asked if she'd be willing to look over my notes and share anything else relevant to her situation.

That's exactly what we did. On her own initiative, Shawna borrowed and read a book about her condition that I'd picked up. She said this was her first chance to see articulated and explained what she had long known through experience. We also found a couple of assessment tools to help further name and classify her experiences.

I believe the collaborative approach of sharing the results of my research with Shawna also served indirectly as a trust-builder. Hopefully, it communicated that I was serious about knowing her and not just labeling her. It was definitely critical for me and gave me a valuable context to understand nuanced interactions that I otherwise would have drastically misinterpreted. It helped me become aware of choices I could make that would create fewer obstacles for Shawna in our relationship.

I may serve at Wellspring as a therapist, but I have learned so much from these beautiful women in return. One of my greatest lessons (and challenges!) has been the importance of patience and pacing in the therapeutic relationship. The women give what they are able to give in disclosing pieces of their history. I accept and support them, name or rename what they're experiencing, and ask questions. As they begin to feel cared for as a person, often over time they are able and willing to reveal more of their past history and inner struggles.

Throughout the therapeutic process, many of the women remark that this is the first time they have even thought about, let alone articulated to others, the entirety of their significant life experiences—the good, the bad, and the ugly. Imagine how absolutely terrifying and amazingly life-giving it is to finally experience the freedom of being authentically known, loved, and validated. No more isolating, shame-filled secrets. No more living with a false sense of self under a cloud of lies, labels, and condemnation. No more burden of

> How life-giving it is to finally experience the freedom of being authentically known, loved, and validated. No more isolating secrets.

believing one must simply "get over" the past. Instead, by taking the time to lay this early therapeutic foundation, we crack the window open to invite powerful rays of hope, healing, and restoration into the dark, secret spaces of a woman's past.

Before a woman can invite another to stand with her, she must first stop trudging through her life long enough to lift her head and take inventory of her surroundings. Allowing the client time to reflect on the journey is not just one element or one task in counseling; it is a vital vehicle for healing. I am amazed and humbled by the courage of these women as they reflect on their lives and share these intimate and painful details with others. In my impatient hunger for healing and restoration, I would much prefer that we jump straight into healthy living—the good news. Yet it is interesting that throughout Scripture we find another model: acknowledge the problem, and then celebrate the solution.

It recently struck me that Paul's pastoral ministry would have been cheapened if his testimony glossed over his shameful past of murdering followers of Christ. Have you thought about this? What if all his writings to the New Testament churches included *only* the most recent truths the Lord revealed to him? What if he never reminded us of the dark stains of sin marking his former life? It is precisely his violent history that made the Lord's transformation of his life so remarkable.

I had no idea how hard it might be for some of our women to reflect accurately on the details of their former lives. I'm genuinely amazed by how the Lord continues to use this slow, painful process to bring about His restoration.

08~ Her Fight for Justice

The legal system can be a daunting obstacle for anyone, but especially so for the girls we serve who have been dealt many injustices. The consequences of seeking justice can be both highly rewarding and deeply devastating. Wellspring Living therapist Mindy Pierce explains some of the issues for the girl and for the counselor.

by Mindy Pierce

The process of pursuing legal justice against the people who have controlled and abused one of our girls can take an incredible emotional toll on her. During the first several months of therapy, a story of abuse, either recent or long past, usually comes to the surface. As a "mandated reporter"—a professional who works with a vulnerable population—I am legally required to report it to the authorities.

I always notify the girl I'm counseling prior to filing that report. Once it's filed, we have a continuous, open discussion regarding what her desires are and whether she wants to move forward with seeking legal justice. I have become increasingly convinced that this discussion is critical in honoring her voice, as well as honoring the Lord's ability to bring justice at the time and in the manner He chooses.

There are many potential reasons to decline a legal course of action. Sometimes the victim, even when the abuse is extensive, does not hold the perpetrator responsible for the abuse. Instead, she believes *she* is responsible and must be held liable in some way. This is also the message she receives when she or one of her friends is caught in prostitution and is punished in a court of law. When this is the case, she may not be ready for this part of the journey.

Also, if a young woman is legitimately concerned for her safety, we must concede the realities of the threat of harm. Filing a protective or restraining order is sometimes impossible because it would disclose to the perpetrator the girl's precise location and may potentially notify the abuser that she is "speaking out" against him or her. Additionally, the result of limited law enforcement resources is that our girls receive only retroactive protection. Police respond to the 911 call only *after* she has been harmed. Girls in these vulnerable situations quickly learn, before stirring up the hornet's nest, that it's worth considering where their help will come from.

While it can be empowering for a woman to feel heard in telling her story, it can be equally disempowering for her to be questioned by law enforcement. Their questions may leave her feeling they doubt her truthfulness. Also, we must consider the potential harm done when she is forced to relive painful, deeply personal, horrifying details, believing that greater good will result from it—only to be told by the law enforcement representative, "Well, I'm sorry. There's nothing we can do. It's really just a case of 'he said, she said.' "

The legal process is also quite lengthy and can stretch far beyond the average stay in our recovery program. Who will support the girl then? Will an ongoing legal case serve as a continual reminder of previous horrors just when she is truly ready to move beyond her past?

And, what are the implications if there *is* a conviction for the perpetrator? What if the abuser does go to jail? How will that affect the girl? Will she feel it's her fault that this person is serving a sentence? How will it affect her family or relationship dynamics if the abuser is a relative? Will others criticize or even ostracize her? And how long will the person be in jail, really? What happens when the abuser gets released? Who is going to protect the woman *then*? These are all complex and potentially dangerous concerns to consider.

On the other hand, there are also potential benefits to pursuing justice. Sometimes this is one way the client is able to fight back and recover a sense of power, voice, and autonomy, when she previously considered herself weak and silent. It may also be an opportunity for law enforcement personnel to listen to her, respect her, and offer help, instead of dismissing her or viewing her as a criminal. As she is exposed to others' perspectives regarding the abuse, it may reinforce truths and add extra weight and dimension to the reality of the abuse, since her understanding is often clouded by lies from the perpetrator.

In situations where a girl has been dismissed, ignored, or called a liar when she talks about her abuse, the process of seeking justice can be redemptive. For the first time, she is given a platform and the opportunity to be heard. She sees a team of people working and fighting for her. She may begin to see that people will believe her. She may begin to hope that actual justice is a possibility.

Two Contrasting Messages

If a client does decide to move forward in pursuing legal justice, the therapist has yet another unique challenge. The attitude and priorities of the therapist through this process can be either helpful or harmful. The client needs to hear, "I believe you. I believe your story. Your story is important. I'm willing to help you communicate it. I can try to help you make sense of a confusing process. I can try to keep you encouraged and moving forward when you reach another roadblock. You are worth fighting for. We'll take all the time in the world until we get to the very bitter end of the justice path. I'm in this for the long haul.

"When you can't find the words, I will do what I can to create space and an environment for you to find them. When you are afraid and tempted to believe old lies, I can name those thoughts as lies and remind you of the truth. When you grow discouraged, I can remind you of your reasons for wanting to do this."

At the same time, an equally important and somewhat conflicting message is just as essential: "Our pursuit of justice does *not* define our relationship and is not a condition for your healing. It is one piece of the puzzle and may be better saved until other pieces have been placed. I will always be as honest and forthcoming as I can about what I think you are ready for and capable of, and about the costs and benefits to you. In the end, I will always defer to your assessment of what you can handle now and what you cannot, because I will not pursue justice at the potential expense of silencing your voice. Although we know the Lord is a just judge and that He loves justice, I cannot guarantee our efforts will result in legal justice for you on this earth. I will desire and pursue justice for you with tenacity, but I refuse to pursue justice in lieu of healing and restoration."

It is worth noting that the Bible is saturated with calls for us to pursue justice for the oppressed (read the Psalms, Proverbs, and Isaiah for further study on God's view of the oppressed and how we are called to action). Interestingly, the Lord isn't telling the oppressed to get up and fight harder for themselves. And He's not telling us to wait and "receive" justice for them. He uses very active language: "Learn to do right! Seek justice, encourage the oppressed. Defend the cause of the fatherless, plead the case of the widow" (Isaiah 1:17).

I love the parable where Jesus exhorts His disciples to not give up in prayer:

> In a certain town there was a judge who neither feared God nor cared about men. And there was a widow in that town who kept coming to him with the plea, "Grant me justice against my adversary."
>
> For some time he refused. But finally he said to himself, "Even though I don't fear God or care about men, yet because this widow keeps bothering me, I will see that she gets justice, so that she won't eventually wear me out with her coming!"
>
> And the Lord said, "Listen to what the unjust judge says. And will not God bring about justice for his chosen ones, who cry out to him day and night? Will he keep putting them off? I tell you, he will see that they get justice, and quickly." (Luke 18:2–8)

To successfully stand with a woman throughout this process requires that we become like that relentless widow. We are called to plead her case before the throne of heaven and with the God who works justice, as well as to tirelessly plead for justice from others on this earth.

Advocate and Pit Bull

When Denelle came to Wellspring, her trauma was evident in her blatant mistrust of the body. She didn't want to be touched. She was afraid to eat. And she always kept her head down, as if someone was pushing her face to the floor.

Because Denelle had been sexually assaulted in another state, law enforcement was involved prior to her arrival at our assessment center. A detective met with her during her first week at the Wellspring home. At this point, Denelle wasn't pursuing legal action for herself but simply responding to the legal process.

After her second interview with the detective, we discussed her level of commitment to participating in the investigation. We explored whether pursuing a legal judgment against her abuser, a family member and high-profile person, was something she wanted and was ready to commit to, and whether this was the right time. We discussed if it would be possible for her to engage in the investigation without feeling defined by it and without feeling like her goal of moving toward restoration would be overshadowed by what would be required of her mentally, emotionally, and psychologically. Denelle decided that pursuing justice was necessary in order for her to have the best opportunity to feel safe in the future. She believed she could balance the demands with her journey toward healing.

In addition to Denelle's ongoing therapy, her participation in Wellspring classes, and her completion of therapeutic homework and focus packets, we spent a significant amount of time talking about the investigation, preparing for interviews, and reassessing whether she indeed wanted to commit to the next step, and the next step, and the next step.

Denelle's case taught me the importance of preparing girls and helping form their expectations in the legal process. In Denelle's interviews with law enforcement, we discovered that mental preparation made a big difference in her level of comfort from the beginning of the interview. For instance, once she mentally prepared for an upcoming interview with a new male FBI agent she'd never met. When I escorted her into the room, she was surprised that we were also joined by a female detective with whom she'd worked previously and by another Wellspring staff member. It was a no-brainer for us that the detective she'd worked with previously and the staff member, who knew more about the case than anyone else, would be important contributors to this interview. But Denelle didn't expect their presence; I hadn't thought to communicate that. The interview was not a great success.

I learned later that Denelle felt she never really recovered from the shock that this interview was not what she'd prepared for. She felt surprised, anxious, and panicked, and we hadn't spent time beforehand practicing self-soothing or relaxation skills for such situations.

We learn from mistakes, of course, and try not to repeat them! Next time, to help Denelle feel better prepared, I did more research on what she could expect. We also practiced coping skills so she would know what to do when she was surprised and started feeling panicky and overwhelmed.

We have spent hours finding ways and words to articulate Denelle's story. One of the our most significant challenges in the legal process is that law enforcement representatives need detailed information about the abuse and trauma, yet they are legally limited to asking open-ended, general questions. They are not allowed to "lead the victim" with their inquiries.

Legal representatives may ask, "What can you tell me about what happened to you?" But when a young woman has been taught to believe that her voice does not matter, that the abuse is her fault, and that speaking out will only result in greater harm for her, she is highly unlikely to answer the question in any detail. Shame and embarrassment cause her to want to disclose as little as possible. She rarely believes anyone would be interested in the details. Unfortunately, she is unaware of how significant some details are for law enforcement. The detective has not developed trust with her and cannot get to those details with the indirect, vague questioning that is legally required.

Our response to this challenge is to ask the woman to write out a statement for the counselor. The counselor can ask questions, gather more details (perhaps from information the girl disclosed during prior sessions), and invite finer points of explanation. The written statement is then given to the investigator, who may come back with more focused questions.

When an FBI agent requested a recorded forensic interview with Denelle, we asked for time to discuss and make the decision. Denelle took time to reflect and write out fears connected with her being recorded. She wrote down possible benefits that might result. She identified truths that would confront the lies and fears she had accumulated. She wrote down questions: Why did she need to be recorded? What was the recording going to be used for? If she was recorded, would that mean that she would not have to appear in court against her abuser?

On Denelle's behalf, I posed these questions directly to the agent. I wrote out the answers and gave them to Denelle, giving her time to reflect and weigh the costs and benefits of being recorded. After some thought, she decided to follow through with the recorded interview. She stayed with this decision even after we learned that the interview would be conducted by an agent from the FBI's national office rather than someone we'd worked with before.

We scheduled the interview, and to practice and prepare, I requested a preliminary walk-through for both Denelle and me and an introduction to the interviewer prior to the day of the interview. I wrote a summary of important considerations for interviewing this client and a rough outline of the extent of the abuse she had shared thus far in the case.

We went for the walk-through, then processed that experience. We discussed again whether Denelle wanted to proceed despite her fears and anxieties. We talked through the reasons for the vague and overwhelming questions from detectives and interviewers, and prepared Denelle as to how she might respond to these questions. We practiced relaxation techniques. She again wrote out her reasons for choosing to move forward with the investigation. We explored possibilities for anything that could help her feel more at ease during the interview. I contacted the interviewer and asked if Denelle could listen to relaxing, peaceful music during the interview, explaining the positive impact such an accommodation might have. The interviewer consulted her supervisors and agreed.

The interview was difficult. It took Denelle days to process it and decompress. Then, the interviewer requested an additional session. We asked Denelle to let us know when she felt ready to go back, which she did, and then we prepared again. I questioned the detectives regarding what information they needed from my client in order to move forward with the case. We went for the second interview and waited to hear from law enforcement. Since the abuser was still at large, we asked to be notified in advance if they were moving forward with an attempt to arrest so that we could take extra security precautions.

Our efforts also included ten months of phone calls, messages, and faxes as we pursued evidence that had been collected after the sexual assault against Denelle almost a year before. We also met with members of the US Attorney's office, communicated with several lawyers agreeing to work on the case pro bono, and networked through a monthly Commercial Sexual Exploitation of Children meeting with law enforcement and medical professionals.

Despite the combined efforts of Denelle, the Wellspring staff, and a host of law enforcement officials, FBI officials decided there was insufficient evidence to bring charges against her abuser. The case has been turned over to authorities in Denelle's home state. We've started over.

Sometimes pursuing justice and standing with the young woman requires playing the part of that relentless widow—not unlike an annoying terrier dog that yaps and yaps. Sometimes, it may even take a little bit of pit bull. No matter what, it always requires intentional advocating and a great deal of patience.

Because It's the Right Thing

After months of therapy, peeling back layers, and building trust, Natalie disclosed an extensive history of childhood abuse by a family perpetrator. She also told me of her concern for her younger sibling, who she believed was at risk by being at the home with the perpetrator. I reported this to a government social services department.

Weeks later, Natalie reported she'd been raped on an overnight visit back home by that same family member. Because the rape happened out of state, we had difficulty securing help from both the assault center and the police in Georgia. This was one of my early opportunities to play the role of annoying terrier.

I hit numerous roadblocks while pursuing help for Natalie. The trail of emails and phone calls was endless, yet despite this, I was rarely able to make contact. The local police station never called me back. The local assault center couldn't talk to us until we took the client to an emergency room. But when we tried to get into the emergency room, the hospital wouldn't admit Natalie without a police report. After jumping all these hurdles, Natalie was finally received by the assault center for an assessment.

I hated dragging Natalie with us through this process because I was afraid that she would learn that girls who speak up about rape are rewarded with messy policies and disregard. I thought, *A broken woman who is ashamed, feels disgusting, and wants to hide—who has been told for years that no one would believe her if she told—is supposed to jump through all these hoops and pursue help and justice for herself?*

No wonder we have such a low reporting rate.

In an effort to see her sibling protected, Natalie agreed to file a statement with the police. Because her rape took place out of state, we did all that we could via phone and fax. Natalie did need to be driven to the sheriff's office in the county where the offense occurred, however, to meet with a detective.

Such a meeting can be emotionally loaded and highly volatile for one of our girls, so the person transporting needs to be someone who knows her and the extent of the abuse, can speak in a way that is helpful and not harmful to the client, and is comfortable advocating for the needs of the client. I believe that whether a therapist, staff member, volunteer, or another primary support person fills this role, if this girl trusts us, we have the unique responsibility and calling to rearrange our schedule and serve her by being with her during each step of this process.

I spent hours of one-on-one time with Natalie, helping her write out her statement. Then the detective requested that she write additional statements about abuse

> Whenever a girl's path toward restoration involves legal matters, we must be prepared to go the extra mile.

from years past. We rode with the detective so Natalie could identify the locations where that abuse had transpired. We made at least two more trips to work with the out-of-state sheriff's office on this case.

It appeared that headway was being made and an arrest was close at hand, but then the situation took a surprising and difficult turn. When some of Natalie's statements didn't make sense, we decided together at Wellspring to ask her to take a lie detector test. It indicated that Natalie had been lying about many things, including the recent report of rape.

She'd chosen to have sex with someone else that weekend and was trying to protect herself from negative consequences.

If I had invested all this time and energy because I was dedicated only to the outcome, I would have been devastated and thoroughly enraged. As it was, I was incredibly disappointed, even angry with Natalie, over her deceit. But because I was committed to the process and to allowing the Lord to work out the outcome, I was able to leave the situation in His hands. This difficult learning experience solidified for me the importance of always doing the right thing for the client simply because we are called to love and serve her well, not because we need to engineer a particular outcome.

The Extra Mile

Whenever a girl's path toward restoration involves legal matters, we must be prepared to go the extra mile. It may mean making more phone calls than we can imagine, sending emails and faxes, advocating, liaising, and even literally driving the extra mile.

One of our staff members once agreed to take Jocelyn to her court appointment to finalize her divorce. Doing so required the staffer to get up at 3 a.m., then pick up Jocelyn at 4 a.m. to drive four and a half hours to the courthouse. The trip meant not only the finalization of the divorce, but also a return to an area where Jocelyn had lived with another abusive man and had worked in local strip clubs. The trip was emotionally daunting as Jocelyn was overwhelmed by memories of her former life and relationships.

After the court session, the Wellspring staffer suggested they go to the beach to pray. She hoped it would help bring closure and would create memories of Jocelyn's new life in Christ. They drove an additional hour to a rock-strewn beach that faced the Atlantic Ocean. There they walked on the sand, worshiped, prayed, and cried.

On the walk back to the car, Jocelyn shook her head. "What a day," she said. "I needed this. Back in the city, I was starting to get that trapped feeling again. But being here"—she waved her arm at the beach and waves—"just reminds me that God is bigger than all of that. Thank you."

For both Jocelyn and the Wellspring staff member, it was a refreshing and renewing time. Over the next several weeks, both reflected on how cleansing the trip was. It was worth it to drive those few extra miles for Jocelyn to go an even greater distance in her healing process.

For me, that is so much of what being a therapist is about—making that extra effort to get to know a girl, help her discover the issues she is facing, and advocate for her whenever and wherever needed so that she can become the woman God intended her to be. This is what I so appreciate about the people I work with. They are dedicated like no others I've seen to the restoration of these girls—no matter what it takes.

09~Healing Comes Full Circle

One of the most wonderful results we see in a person who has recovered from sexual abuse is her new ability and passion to give back to those who are still caught in despair. Angela, a Wellspring volunteer, understands better than most what our girls are going through.

I've always been a Georgia girl. I wish I could say that life in "The Peach State" has been easy and smooth, but that is simply not the case. I was five years old when a sixteen-year-old cousin locked me in his room on at least two occasions, forcing me to do things, some of them painful, none of which I understood. These events were so confusing and frightening that I blocked them out of my mind. I tried to go on as if it had never happened.

Then, when I was twelve, it happened again. This time it was a neighbor, the older brother of one of my best friends. It's a terrifying feeling when something happens against your will, especially when you know exactly how it is going to end. You have no control over it. You don't know what to do. This neighbor's abuse brought back all the frightening memories I'd buried of being molested when I was five.

I was old enough by now to realize that this was wrong, but I was afraid to say anything. In this limited logic, I believed that if this kept happening to me, it must somehow be my fault. And who would I tell? My father worked two jobs to support our family of five plus two invalid grandparents who lived with us. I rarely saw him. My mother was around, but she was a complex woman, unaffectionate and almost impossible to please. She raised my siblings and me to avoid difficult topics, making conversations about sex completely out of the question. Sharing such a painful and sensitive issue with her was definitely not an option.

I finally found the courage to tell my eleven-year-old friend, the sister of the boy who molested me. She dismissed the whole idea.

"Oh, you're just being ridiculous," she said. "My brother would never do anything like that."

After that, I decided it was better to keep these terrible secrets to myself. What was the point of telling people if no one would believe me?

I didn't talk about what had happened and pretended that it had no effect on me, but silently I felt ashamed, guilty, and dirty. My self-esteem was nonexistent. When I got to high school, I was so shy and withdrawn that I didn't want anyone to look at me. I wanted to be invisible, perhaps because I thought it would protect myself from the unwanted attention of the past. But it didn't work. And when a boy at school tried to take advantage of me, it just reinforced all the poisonous ideas already at work in my head. *I must be a bad person,* I thought. *Something's wrong with me that makes boys react to me this way. I don't know what it is, but it's something, and it's my fault.*

High school became a blur of emotions, anger, confusion, and rebellion. I began dabbling in drugs and developed an eating disorder. For me, it was a way to finally have control of my body and environment. I lost weight and was down to a hundred pounds. Even my usually detached mother was concerned.

At home, I spent much of my time taking care of my younger siblings and sick grandparents. I couldn't wait to escape. When I turned eighteen, I found an office job and moved out.

Then I met a boy through my church youth group who was different. He quickly became my solace, someone I believed would rescue me from the pain I felt, and we started dating. By the age of twenty, I was married and pregnant. Six months into my pregnancy, my father died suddenly and unexpectedly from a heart attack. It was a shock no one in my family was prepared for.

Within a year and a half, my mother met and married a man she'd known only a few months. By this time I was pregnant with my second child. I held on to the fantasy that my life was together. I did all the "right" things—took care of my husband and children, went to church. But I was still suffering from deep emotional pain.

But my silent suffering reached a fever pitch when my sister came to me and said that our stepfather had raped her. This time, there would be no disbelieving or burying of secrets. I took her to the police station so she could report it, and my stepfather was arrested and eventually went to prison. Nevertheless, it was only after my sister passed a lie detector test and submitted to a psychiatric evaluation that my mother believed her and finally filed for divorce.

My own marriage was also unraveling. I discovered that my husband was using drugs and being unfaithful to me. My kids and I moved back home with my mother. My life was falling apart.

How Could He Love Me?

When I was a child, my family attended a small Southern Baptist church. I remember at the age of ten discussing a plan to walk down the aisle one Sunday at church to pray with my pastor. Then my mother said we wouldn't be going that day. I was so disappointed. I knelt by my bed, prayed the sinner's prayer, and asked Jesus to come into my heart. The next Sunday was a bicentennial service. We all put on dresses from that era. In my *Little House on the Prairie* dress, bonnet, braided pigtails, buckteeth, and glasses, I marched to the front of the church and announced that I'd accepted Christ and wanted to be baptized. A week later, I was.

I always knew that God was there. I always believed that Jesus died on the cross for sinners. But I found it difficult to accept His love personally. I felt dirty and unworthy. How could He love me after I'd done these things?

It was when my first marriage began to disintegrate that I started to cry out to God. I sought Him through His Word like never before. I went to counseling and finally revealed the sexual abuse and pain. God began to heal my hurt and help me understand that what had happened to me was not my fault. He opened my eyes to so many truths about His love.

When our marriage got rough, my husband and I even started seeing a Christian counselor. We reconciled for a time, but then he began falling back into his old patterns. He was diagnosed as manic-depressive, and during these bouts he became irrational and sometimes threatening. After much heartache and prayer, I finally decided it was enough. My children and I had to get out of there for our own safety. The divorce was ugly and bitter. There were nights when I feared for my life and the children's lives. My now ex-husband struggled with his illness for three years until my kids were nine and six years old, and then he committed suicide.

This became the darkest period of my life. I had never known such despair. I was depressed and felt utterly alone. I was also angry with

God. How could He allow this to happen to my kids? I didn't want to go on, but I knew my children needed me.

I met a man who seemed the opposite of my first husband. He loved kids and was willing to take us on. Once again, I viewed him as a rescue, an escape from the pit I had fallen into. We married, but it wasn't long before it became obvious that we'd made a mistake. He was deeply insecure and became jealous over my continual promotions at work. He competed with the kids for my attention and became another child to take care of instead of a partner and mate. When I tried to work things out or urge him to go to counseling with me, he refused. Finally, I couldn't take it anymore, so I filed for divorce. Once again, I had hurt my children. Once again, I had failed.

I was broken and desperate. I was also right where I needed to be for God to break through.

I searched my heart and looked back at my life and the choices I'd made. I began letting go of the anger and blame I'd placed on God. I started seeking Him again and praying for guidance. I was so down that I was finally willing to let Him pick me up. It was as if He were saying to me, "C'mon, Angela, you're not done. It's not over for you. I love you as I always have."

Slowly, I began to break free from the bondage that had held me under for so many years. I continued to push forward and eventually got to a point where I felt strong—strong in my faith, strong in my career, strong in who I was as an individual and a mother.

Little did I know that God wasn't finished with me yet.

A Heart on Fire

It was 2005 and I was happy for the first time I could remember. At work, things were incredibly busy. Over the previous few years I'd worked alongside my boss, partnering with Mark to manage a large mortgage banking division. Serving together as the regional president and vice president of operations, Mark and I became friends through it all.

Then Mark asked me to a dinner. A personal request, not a professional function.

I panicked. I had a terrible track record with men, and I was scared to venture out again. But I gave it some prayerful consideration and decided that if this was to be, God would show me the way. I insisted we begin our relationship with Christian counseling. I'd decided that an ounce of prevention was definitely worth a pound of cure, and I would not enter into another relationship unless I knew it was built on the right foundation. Mark agreed, so we began counseling and dating. We uncovered a lot of baggage through the counseling process, but through many tears and prayers, we grew together in healing, trust, and communication skills that I had never before experienced.

Today, Mark and I have been married for more than five years. I can truly say I have found the man God intended for me. He is my best friend, my partner, my soul mate. We have a healthy, loving marriage that I can only attribute to the fact that it is founded in Christ. I finally feel like I did something right! Through all my adversity, God has refined, tempered, and molded me. He has also taught me so much about the effects of abuse—which is never pleasant to experience firsthand—but I believe it is part of His unexpected plan for me to reach out to others who have had similar experiences.

When a large corporation purchased our company three years ago, I decided to give up my job. I had no idea what to do with myself, so I prayed for God to give me direction. I sensed Him urging me to get involved in something where I could give back, perhaps some type of charity work, but I had no idea how to find what I was looking for. When six months of searching went by, I felt discouraged. Though I feared it would be boring, I allowed myself to be talked into signing up for a golf clinic. During lunch at the club one day, I met a woman who volunteered for an organization called Wellspring Living. When I asked her what kind of group it was, she told me that their mission was to restore the lives of women who were sexually abused as children.

Immediately, my heart felt like it was on fire! I knew that was what God had been leading me to. I couldn't wait to get involved.

My volunteer work for Wellspring has included providing transportation for the girls, volunteering in the Wellspring Treasures store, taking on Christmas projects, asking for donations, helping with fashion shows, and just being a friend to the girls and

> "No matter what happened to you, God is bigger than that. He can heal you and walk you through to the other side. I'm a living testament that you can get better."

women in the program. One of the first things I agreed to do was serve as a substitute teacher in a class of four women for six weeks. When they told me the first class was called "How Does Jesus View Sex?" I thought, *You're kidding me.* I was a recovering wallflower with zero teaching experience, and could not believe my first teaching day would involve this sensitive and potentially explosive topic. But this was where God had put me, and uncomfortable or not, I was going to do my best.

In that first class, I asked the women, "What's your first memory of sex?" They all started to cry. One talked about what her father did when she was five years old. Another spoke about what an uncle did when she was nine.

"I understand," I said. "That was my first memory as well. But it doesn't always have to hurt this way. This isn't what God intended. No matter what happened to you, God is bigger than that. He can heal you and walk you through to the other side. I'm a living testament that you can get better."

I noticed that one of the women, a mom in her thirties who was new to the program, was listening to me intently. "But how did you get over it?" she asked.

"God helped me get over it," I said. "It's a journey. I had to start trusting and walking with Him."

She shook her head at me. "Well, I was a prostitute and a crack-head. I was on the streets."

"All I can say is that He can deliver you. You have a choice now. You do not have to be the victim anymore. You can choose to let Him heal you."

The woman slowly nodded her head. She was thinking about it.

I didn't expect my words to instantly change her life. But I hoped I'd planted a seed, one that would continue to be cultivated in the days and years ahead.

Unconditional Love

Because God had broken through to me with His unconditional love, I was able to help Shelby, a struggling girl in our Wellspring program, to also encounter this great love. Shelby was in her twenties, with long, dark hair she sometimes seemed to hide behind. During her first year in the program, she was always polite to me, but distant. Then one night she approached and said she'd like to spend more time with me.

"Shelby, I'd love that," I said. "Why don't you call me sometime when you'd like to get together?"

Shelby looked down at the ground for a moment. "I'm used to people saying that," she said. "But then they never really follow through."

"Give me a try."

A few weeks later, Shelby did call, asking if I could help her look for an apartment. We spent the entire day together, along with my husband, exploring the area and getting to know each other. It wasn't long before a new bond formed. I remember talking to Mark that night about how much I admired Shelby for how far she'd come in her journey. We were both amazed at her ability to face things head-on, taking a practical and fearless approach to everyday challenges like work, finances, and finding a place to live.

We did find Shelby an apartment that day, and she moved in about three weeks later. I'd like to report that Shelby's life changed for the better in a steadily rising line, but it wasn't nearly that easy. She had transportation issues that left her dependent on others and caused her to miss church. She continued to struggle with the sexual abuse in her past and the on-and-off battle with anorexia and bulimia over the years. She said she never really felt loved growing up.

"God loves you and I love you, unconditionally," I said. "You are a beautiful person with a beautiful heart and a lot to give. I'm certain God has a purpose for you. You need to work to get better so you can use what you've learned to help others."

Shelby began to cry. "I've never felt love like you've shown me!" she said. "You're like the mom I always wanted."

"I never understood that they really loved me . . . even though I failed them. They love me unconditionally!"

But self-destructive patterns can be difficult to give up, and Shelby's struggles with eating disorders continued. Her body declined to the point that she entered the hospital several times before checking into a state mental facility. Two months later, the doctors determined that

Shelby was stabilized and ready for release, but she'd lost her job and her apartment. She had nowhere to go. The staff at Wellspring Living stepped in, arranging to bring Shelby back to the assessment center where she could stay and regain her footing.

For Shelby, this was a revelation. "I never understood that they really loved me," she said. "Wellspring has proven to me that they really do love me, even though I failed them. They love me unconditionally!"

After some soul-searching, Shelby returned to her mother's house while waiting to be accepted into an eating disorder clinic. We still text each other daily and talk frequently. I thank God for joining our paths together. I know He has a plan and purpose for Shelby, just like He has a purpose for me. I'm excited to see where God takes both of us.

Although Shelby's journey isn't over, she's reached a place in her heart that allows her to give and receive love in a healthy way. I know exactly how she feels. Overcoming sexual abuse is not easy, but with God, it *is* possible.

10~ We Must Build Trust

To a girl who has been betrayed by people she should be able to trust, anyone who looks handsome, pretty, or put-together spells danger. From her experience, someone who appears respectable is often pretending. Appearances are rarely what they seem.

The typical story of a Wellspring girl is that someone she trusted, usually a family member or friend, stole her innocence by the time she was eight years old, abusing her emotionally, physically, and sexually. Maybe he even took her words and twisted them to make her look bad. During and after the abuse, the abuser said he cared and that he was there to help, but instead he brought only pain. He may have been her father or boyfriend. The first social lesson that victims of abuse learn is that people who proclaim good intentions may actually hurt them the most.

It's far easier for one of our girls to trust someone who doesn't look put-together than to trust someone who comes to her knowing all the answers. One girl eloquently put it this way: "I'm only asking for a consistent, authentic, and intentional relationship, along with time to prove that your life is what it seems and your intentions are pure. I need those things to be congruent, and you can't show me that overnight."

Kelly is a young woman who built a relationship based on trust with Haley, a teen who had been sexually abused by her stepfather and had been pulled into the world of sex trafficking. When they met, neither was part of Wellspring, but that was destined to change. Here is their story, as told by Haley.

A New Friend

I first met Kelly on a hot summer day at our apartment complex pool. At the time, I was seventeen. Kelly was twenty-three. I had stretched out on a lounge chair, working on my tan, when she jumped out of the pool and toweled off in a chair next to me. She started talking to me, asking questions, just being friendly. We ran into each other a couple more times at the pool. Pretty soon Kelly was inviting me to join her on grocery shopping trips and even a fast-food lunch.

I was sure she had an ulterior motive. I couldn't understand why she treated me like a friend since it seemed she had plenty already, but she did. I don't trust easily because of what's happened to me in the past. Everyone who's shown any interest in me has ended up using me, so I just waited for the same thing to happen with Kelly. But that day never came.

When she first told me to call her, I thought, *She's crazy. I'll never share with her what's really going on in my life.* I was quiet and reserved with Kelly, but she just accepted me as I was and hung out with me. No expectations.

Kelly was a fun-loving person. She experienced joy in every little thing. When I was around her, I couldn't help but smile, something I rarely did otherwise. She checked in on me throughout the week to be sure I was okay. She learned that I lived with my sister, which was crazy for me because Lisa and her husband were high all the time. They both had terrible tempers too. I was always afraid of saying or doing the wrong thing around them.

Little by little, I began to understand that Kelly truly cared for me and that it was safe to tell her what I was going through. Only a few weeks before, after over a year of living in an apartment with five other girls and being forced to have sex with men every day, I'd finally escaped. I was hiding at my sister's apartment, afraid every day that my pimp would find me.

One day, alone at my sister's apartment, I called Kelly and opened up to her more. She was there. She listened.

"The worst part is the nightmares," I said. "I keep seeing their faces . . . all those men, looking at me like I'm cattle or something. I can never seem to get away from them."

Kelly didn't condemn me or treat me like I was a freak. She also didn't try to fix me. She was unlike anyone else I knew, and I began to wonder if this was because she was a Christian. Her friendship offered me a new look at a Christian who truly cared and was real about not only my struggles but also hers. She'd had her own problems in the past. She and her mom didn't get along at all. Her mom had tried to control her so intensely that Kelly ran away from home.

Authenticity is a rare commodity, and just as valuable. It's much easier to be vulnerable and honest with someone when you feel he or she is being vulnerable and honest with you.

Because Kelly was sincere about getting to know who I was, my favorite food (pizza), favorite drink (caramel macchiato at Starbucks), my quirks (biting my fingernails), and my talents (I used to sing in a school choir), I began trusting her more. She wasn't so shocked or fixated on my trauma that she stopped seeing the person that I was. She helped me to find hope in the reality that my background didn't define me. She helped me see that the person God created me to be wasn't dead, that there was life still inside of me.

Kelly was always giving—in both big ways and small. It was the little things she did that kept us connected—like shooting me a text or bringing me dinner. Sometimes we just sat around together in silence. It was so comforting to know that I didn't have to "perform" for her or become someone I wasn't. She accepted me just as I am, bringing out my strengths and celebrating my interests. When she found out that I love animals, she and I went to the zoo. We couldn't afford to do that too often, so sometimes we just went to the pet store!

Because Kelly helped me peel away these thick walls I'd built around me, I began to have a small ray of hope for the future.

I was amazed to see that Kelly continued to stand and share life with me even though I had nothing to offer her. I was like an unanchored ship at sea, rising and falling on the water. One day I'd treat her well, the next I might ignore her calls or not talk when we were together. No matter what, she stayed true.

After we'd been friends for a few months, not much had changed in terms of my fears. I was still suspicious of the world, still stressed about living with my sister, and still afraid I'd be found by my pimp. I know it was hard for Kelly to see me like that. She told me about a place called Wellspring Living, a program for teens like me who needed to get away and have a fresh start. It sounded great and terrifying at the same time. Put my life into the hands of strangers? I didn't think so.

Kelly didn't push it. She didn't try to force me to change. She wanted my life to be different, but she was willing to wait until I began to see that a different life was actually an option.

One night at my sister's apartment, I realized that "different" might be a better option than what I was living. During dinner with my sister and her husband, I dropped a water glass on the floor and it shattered, and with it, any remaining sense of security I had. My sister's husband went crazy. I think he had been drinking.

"You're going to pay for that!" he yelled, pushing me against the wall. I got out of there as fast as I could.

In tears, I called Kelly. I had no one else to turn to, at least no one I felt I could trust. I explained what had happened. "Can I stay with you tonight?" I asked.

"Haley, of course," she said. "Let me come get you."

We talked for a long time that night. I went back and forth between crying, feeling scared, and feeling angry. I knew I couldn't keep living like this. Something had to change.

"You know that place, Wellspring?" I said. "I'm thinking about giving them a call."

Kelly just nodded, and smiled.

Just a few weeks later, I joined the Wellspring Living Girls' Program, and as I look back, I mark this as the point that began my journey into healing. I was thrilled when Kelly soon joined Wellspring as a staff member responsible for furnishing a new home for girls in the program.

Looking back, I am so glad Kelly was willing to wait for me to decide that I was ready to change. I'm so thankful she remained a consistent friend. Without her example, I don't think I would have trusted anyone enough to reach out for recovery.

An Authentic Relationship

The need to establish trust is reinforced every time I meet a new girl or woman who enters Wellspring Living. Trust is very difficult to establish because many times it is her mom or dad or uncle or cousin who abused or exploited her. When the very people a young girl should be able to trust violate her, how can she believe that a stranger has good intentions and will walk with her through recovery? This is the challenge we face every day.

Building trust certainly isn't an easy process. There is no formula that guarantees any of our girls will ever cross that line to accept it. To a victim of abuse, every new relationship is a risk, and gaining trust takes time and consistent demonstrations of compassion. Trust grows through authentic, unselfish relationships, relationships that focus on the other person's needs.

> When we are in the height of hopelessness, God reaches out to us. . . . He is the one who makes the first move and who rescues us.

Think about how God relates to us. When we are in the height of hopelessness, it is God who reaches out to us. When we don't feel we have the strength to seek Him, it is God who pursues us. It is God who surprises us in His provision for us. He is the one who makes the first move and who rescues us.

In a similar way, we at Wellspring actively pursue a relationship with our girls. It's not so that we can say we have "rescued" a girl, or even that we've brought her to faith. The reason we pursue reaching out to the hurting is that we sense a call to the individual and to God. We are being obedient to God by following His nudge to get to know this person who we see is hurting. In reaching out, we must stay in a place of prayer and seek God for His plans and purposes for the relationship. If we do that, we will begin the journey because we are following Christ, not a cause.

Our biggest challenge in remaining authentic is having no expectations of the person we've been called to help. It is vital that we demonstrate that we care about the girls we are serving, and not merely their progress or success in the recovery program. We can't let a negative response or a relapse deter us from offering our unconditional love.

We must get past her suspicions and get to know her in a way that touches the depths of her heart.

One of my favorite names for God is Emmanuel, meaning "He is with us." God's statement "Never will I leave you; never will I forsake you" (Hebrews 13:5) gives us a model for our relationship with our girls, showing that a consistent presence is vital. To build trust, we must be there for her and make ourselves available for conversation and practical provisions, and always offer ourselves as a listening ear. Just as God patiently waits for us, we should patiently demonstrate unconditional love.

However, there are precautions—we don't want to become enablers. I encourage our staff and volunteers, before they meet with one of the girls, to pray and ask God to show them what He wants them to do and say. God is wonderful in that He loves us at the same time that He reveals healthy boundaries. In the same way, the authentic, unconditional love we give to the girls at Wellspring also confronts and sets boundaries. The goal isn't to get her to love us, but for her to choose to love God and live a restored life forever. In view of this all-important goal, we must let go of any expectation of being her best friend. She may not ever appreciate our commitment to always be there for her. Yet when we consistently reach out to her, speaking the truth in love, meeting her needs without enabling destructive behavior, we can build a healthy relationship that may lead her into healing.

Allowing God to teach us how to be intentional in relationships can also build our own intimacy with the Lord. Recognizing that we are helpless without His guidance brings us to a place of constant prayer, compelling us to rely on Him for every next step.

Jesus was personal and intentional with each person He interacted with. In His earthly ministry, He seemed to ignore everyone else so He could focus on the person with whom He was engaged, and I believe

He gives us this same undivided attention today. One of the sweetest things about my relationship with God is that He knows just what I need and provides it in the most unique and timely manner. Receiving an unexpected blessing, one that I hadn't even thought to ask Him for, shows me that He is intentional and personal. He knows just what I need to reaffirm His love for me, just as He knows exactly how to communicate His love to hurting young women (www.thewhiteumbrella campaign.com/video/#Stories).

In the same way, we try to bless the girls who so desperately need love and a friend they can trust.

11~ We Must Do Whatever It Takes

Jenn McEwen has been on the Wellspring Living staff since 2004. Her heart is selflessly dedicated to the girls and women we serve. Her story of doing whatever it takes for Maria is inspiring proof that recovery is messy but filled with second chances.

By Jenn McEwen

When I first met Maria three years ago, I wasn't quite sure what to make of her. We'd recently opened the girls program for victims of sex trafficking, and one of my responsibilities was to teach a class on spiritual development. Maria was an outspoken seventeen-year-old in my class who distracted the group one moment and asked insightful questions about God's role in her life the next. Though I could tell there was something deeper going on behind the intimidating and erratic behavior, I wasn't sure what it was.

Maria was tall—close to six feet. When she walked into the room, she was a formidable presence, both physically and socially. With a single comment, she could draw the group into our scheduled activity or hijack the class altogether. Her influence was undeniable.

The week before Thanksgiving, I attended a meeting in which our staff discussed plans for each girl for the holiday. Maria came up in our discussion, as we were concerned for her. While in the program, each of the girls is required to stay in the program's community home created for up to fourteen young women. On Thanksgiving Day, nearly all the girls would be visited by their families. Maria's family, however, wasn't coming.

It's difficult for most to be away from family around the holidays, but it's a different situation for a teenage girl who'd spent the last three years held hostage in an apartment, with no friends and barely enough to eat, where she was forced to have sex with strangers. So I volunteered to bring Maria lunch on Thanksgiving Day and spend time with her while the other girls visited with their families. It would be a chance to get to know this intriguing girl a little better.

I asked Maria what type of food she'd like me to bring, expecting she would want turkey and dressing or some other comfort food. To my surprise, her request was Chinese food. *Chinese food?* A few days before the holiday, I called every Chinese restaurant in the area. Lo and behold, they would all be closed on Thanksgiving Day. Who wants Chinese food on Thanksgiving?

Unwilling to risk disappointing a girl who already felt the pain of her family's absence, I picked up Maria's order the day before and put it in my refrigerator. Even though I was a poor replacement for her mother and siblings, I would do my best.

When I arrived on Thanksgiving Day, some of the other girls' families were already there visiting, and the home was bustling with people and food. While waiting for Maria, I prepared our nonntraditional meal in one of the rooms where we have classes. When Maria finally arrived, I greeted her and stood to give her a hug. She seemed glad to see me, but even more eager to see what I had brought with me.

"Do you have the Chinese food you said you'd bring?"

When I handed over the meal, a smile crept across her face. She dug right in.

We watched children from other families run around the room as we ate. I tried to make small talk.

"So what made you want Chinese food for Thanksgiving?" I said. "I was surprised when I heard that's what you wanted."

"I dunno," Maria said between bites. "It's good."

Our conversation was awkward and filled with silences, and after our hour together was over, I wouldn't say we became best friends. But it was worth it to make this genuine step toward getting to know each other better, even over something as simple as a shared meal.

Maria Goes to College

Maria and I continued to get to know each other through my discipleship class, and before I knew it, Maria was nearing the end of her time in the program. I still wasn't completely sure who she was behind her extroverted behaviors, but she had become special to me. One thing I had learned was that she was smart and fiercely independent.

Maria had worked hard to fulfill her high school grade requirements and make up the credits that had been lost due to skipping classes and a lack of effort. Through her educational experience in the girls program, she proved to herself that she was smart enough to succeed. In fact, she did so well in school and earned so many credits that she was graduating with her high school diploma at the same time she was graduating from the therapeutic program. I was so proud of all of her progress. I really believed she had the potential to rise above all she'd experienced. All she needed was another chance.

The entire program staff began working on Maria's plan to transition out of the program. Because of her good performance at school, we began to look into options for college. We also wanted her to have a stable place to live while she continued her education, so we did some research and found an entry program at a college in South Georgia. There was a huge list of things that needed to be accomplished if Maria wanted to go, and our staff helped Maria work through the list and decisions she needed to make, one by one.

Maria threw herself diligently into college preparations. She studied for the SAT, filled out the college application, tracked down the information needed to apply for financial aid, and even applied for a few scholarships. It was a massive undertaking, but all her hard work paid off when we got the good news—she had been accepted! Now, we just needed to figure out how to pay for it.

> It was hard to tell who was more excited—Maria, who was thrilled at her chance to attend college, or our staff, who had witnessed her transform from disruptive girl to young woman headed toward a bright college career.

It was absolutely amazing to see things come together for Maria. A family foundation in the community stepped forward and generously offered Maria a scholarship to attend for her first year of school. If she achieved good grades, the scholarship was renewable for three more years. She was very excited and very nervous. We took trips down to the campus twice, once for a campus tour and a second time for student orientation. It was well worth four hours of driving each way to see Maria fulfilling her potential and overcoming her past traumas.

During our time together, Maria and I talked about balancing schoolwork and fun, choosing friends and dating relationships wisely, going to class each day, securing a job for spending money, and understanding that I was here for her and all she had to do was reach out if she had trouble. However, I could tell from these conversations that Maria lacked some of the life skills that were necessary to succeed at college. When we made college visits, I was able to build a relationship with the director of Maria's program, and I kept that line of communication open so that I had someone I could check in with at the school.

Maria didn't have the items she needed for a dorm room, so we hosted a going-to-college shower, complete with a registry for her at a local store. Members from the community purchased items on her behalf and sent them to us. At the party we presented Maria with the gifts, her scholarship, and a laptop for her to use at school as a gift from the scholarship foundation. It was hard to tell who was more excited—Maria, who was thrilled at her chance to attend college, or our staff, who had witnessed the transformation from the disruptive girl in class to a young woman headed toward a bright college career.

Missing Classes

At the end of the summer, Maria's family drove her down to South Georgia and moved her into her dorm room. Once in school, Maria talked on the phone with us at least daily, and the message I heard from her was that things were going great. She had set her dorm room up with all her new belongings. She was well-stocked with brightly colored corkboards, school supplies, snacks, and dorm room goodies.

Imagine my surprise when the director of the program called to say Maria had already missed several classes, and it was only the first week of school. The director said she had scheduled a meeting with Maria on Monday and that she would let me know how things went. I called Maria. No answer. I emailed Maria. No answer. I Skyped Maria. No answer. I knew something was not right.

After not hearing from Maria all weekend, I decided I also would meet with the director on Monday. To make the 9 a.m. meeting, I had to leave at five that morning. I sat outside the director's office waiting for them both to arrive. Other students streamed past, but there was no sign of Maria.

Finally, at almost 9:20, Maria waltzed around the corner, looking like she'd just rolled out of bed and smelling like she'd found time for a cigarette on the way. We met with the director, and she cautioned Maria that these types of absences would quickly lead to failure at the school. It was important that Maria attend her classes.

"Maria, I know what a talented person you are, and that you've overcome so much," I said. "You know how important it is to go to class and make your grades. Can you help me understand why you wouldn't go to class?"

Maria didn't want to look at me or the director. "I don't know," she mumbled. "I don't know."

The meeting ended, but I still had no idea why Maria was skipping classes. Surely she understood how important this was.

We walked back to her dorm room together, neither of us saying a word. Finally, her head still down, her voice barely a whisper, Maria spoke.

"Ms. Jenn, I don't know how to get there. I don't know where the classes are."

I was shocked. "Maria, why didn't you just ask someone?"

"It's never been okay for me to ask for help," she said. "It was always a really bad thing."

My heart was broken. Who would have thought that simply requesting help would be so overwhelming? Maria had struggled through several days of orientation yet didn't feel comfortable enough, even with me, to ask for assistance. It made me realize the depth of her wounds; she would need more support than we originally thought.

It turned out Maria didn't know where the cafeteria was, either. She had spent two weeks eating the snacks we'd purchased for her dorm room before she left home.

Following our talk, I walked with Maria around campus and gave her the grand tour. I showed her where to find all her classrooms, the cafeteria, and the local grocery store, where we replenished some of her supplies. Then she had to go to class.

Significant Support

After that trip, I visited Maria twice a month. I felt she wouldn't be able to move forward without significant support; I did not feel it was my place to tell anyone else about her traumatic past. This was a new start for her, and I didn't want to force her to expose challenges perhaps better left in the past.

Each time I visited, I tried to help Maria to plug in to this new community. We visited the campus counselor's office and met the counselor, hoping Maria would feel more comfortable going to her. We met with the academic director to talk about her progress in school. We met with a mentor I was able to link Maria to through some of my own personal contacts. These initial meetings always went well, but Maria seemed paralyzed when it became time to follow through after I was gone. I even tried to set her up with a tutor because we realized that she was struggling in her classes, especially in math. The tutor was a spitfire, eager to take Maria on and help her succeed. After being stood up several times, however, the tutor decided it wasn't a good fit.

I didn't always feel like a welcome visitor, either. I might confirm with Maria a day or two ahead about my plans to drive down, but when I got there about noon and called Maria on my cell phone, there was no answer. There were at least two times I stood outside the locked dorm building door and waited for someone to exit so I could get in. Even her hall had a locked door. Trying to not look like a stalker, I waited for someone to leave so I could slip in and knock on her door, wondering if I'd made the trip for nothing. Maria would finally stumble to the door and say something like "I overslept" or "I forgot you were coming."

Without any comment, I'd say, "Are you ready to go out for lunch?" I think that was Maria's favorite part about my visits. She had difficulty getting the job we'd planned on, so she didn't have much spending money. Going out to eat was a treat. I always let her choose where and what she wanted.

On every visit, I felt it was important to talk to Maria about how much potential she had and how much I believed in her. It was true! There was no room for conversations about her lack of appreciation or respect for my time or my commitment to her. The fact is, I was spending time with her, and it was time for me to encourage her. She didn't get the message that she was special anywhere else. She never heard others say that she was smart, and that if she made wise choices, she could do whatever she wanted to do. Because I had only a short amount of time with her, I wanted the main message she heard from me to be about hope and her ability to change her future.

> I wanted the main message she heard from me to be about hope and her ability to change her future.

It wasn't easy with Maria, but I knew that after all she'd been through, Maria needed time to develop understanding and empathy. I also wondered that she might be testing me to see if I really cared or not.

There were many times when I didn't know if what I was doing for Maria made any difference to her. I wasn't sure that the huge amount of time and energy I poured into the relationship was accomplishing anything. I knew, however, that if I didn't do it, no one would.

A New Second Chance

I had conversations with Maria that I never thought I'd have—about making wise choices, managing money, and birth control. It was, however, exactly what she needed.

Then she called and said she'd gotten into an altercation on campus. The campus police had filed a charge. On my next trip down, we went to the campus safety office, spoke with the officers, and got a copy of the incident report. They informed us that Maria had to appear in city court.

Maria's mom had planned to accompany Maria to the court date, but at the last minute, Maria's mom decided not to come and Maria told me she was going to try to go alone. I was not convinced this was a good choice, so I made the trip down to be supportive of her. At that point, it looked like she was not going to make the grades necessary to stay at school with her scholarship. I tried to help her make a plan for what was next. She was unwilling to move back closer to home, however, as she'd begun dating a boy.

I was frustrated with Maria, but I knew that if I didn't help, she was on her own.

I had seen Maria light up in the classroom, I was confident in her ability to do well in college, and I wasn't willing to accept anything less for her.

After the semester ended, I tried to make it clear that no matter what choices Maria made, I still believed in her ability to make good choices and that if she decided to do something, she had unlimited potential. I tried to express that I wanted to be there for her. Though the phone calls and trips slowed down, we still stayed in touch.

It was difficult for me to see Maria going from place to place with her boyfriend. They lived with her boyfriend's father. Then they moved in with his mother. Then they moved in with some of Maria's family. I knew she was not making decisions that would lead her toward the future she wanted, but I also learned the hard way that the decisions were still hers to make. I knew her desire was to get an education and to become stable and independent, but she was the only one who could make the choices to get her there.

After months of checking in, I knew Maria was getting more desperate to find a job and get back into school. She believed that was the only way for her to reach her goals. In our conversations, we spoke more and more about the idea of her coming into the Wellspring home for women. She'd have more independence than she had in the girls program, and would receive counseling and life skills training. But Maria had been in programs for so long, she just wasn't interested anymore. She didn't want to give up her freedom and living with her boyfriend.

It was a heart-wrenching choice. Yet one day Maria decided to reenter the program. It was in her own time and a choice she fully owned. She called me to tell me she was ready, and I made one more four-hour drive to get her. We talked all the way back about her making good choices and about how proud I was of her for choosing to do what was hard in the short-term but much wiser in the long-term. It was hard for me to see her hurt in moving away from her boyfriend, yet it was not pain for the sake of pain. It was pain that was leading her toward a better life.

Now, after several months in the women's program, Maria has stabilized and is making wise decisions. She did not return to her college, but I had the pleasure recently of taking her to a local technical college so that she could turn in her application. No one had to help her put this application together; she did it all by herself. As we were sitting with the representative from the college, the woman remarked, "You are so organized." Both Maria and I beamed with pride.

It took time, but Maria was learning to take the initiative to change her future. I'm so glad I kept with her long enough to see it happen. Just yesterday, she sat in my office on the phone with a representative of the college. After she hung up, I could see by her expression that the news was good.

"I got in!" she yelled. "I got in!"

I am so proud of Maria. Sometimes it takes several tries for a person to find their path, but if the people around her believe in her, it will happen. This is Maria's new second chance. This is her time.

12~ We Will Face Obstacles

The work of intersecting with broken lives is filled with wonderful blessings, but it is not without obstacles. At Wellspring Living, we spent five months repairing and updating an unused facility that would serve girls rescued from the sex trade. We invested great effort to make sure their new home would reflect their worth in God's eyes and at the same time be a place that would become a safe refuge from their perpetrators.

And now, we couldn't wait until all these empty rooms were filled with new faces—new girls we could love and serve in their journey into healing.

I'll never forget the October morning when my phone rang as I pulled into a parking garage. It was Jay, the juvenile justice placement officer for the state of Georgia, calling to tell me in excited terms that a victim of commercial sexual exploitation was ready to be placed in Wellspring Living. She would be the first trafficked young woman to enter our program. After much preparation and hard work, the program was underway.

What should have been a day filled with joy and hope, however, would soon become one of the darkest of my life. Later that same day I received the news that my husband, Dick, had been diagnosed with acute myelogenous leukemia—my strong, wonderful husband now had a life-threatening disease.

I was devastated. Dick had always been my sounding board, my encourager, and my prayer warrior, and I couldn't imagine life without him. The news of both of these events together was overwhelming. One was good news, the other, horrifying. I had to tell Jay that he would have to call someone else in the organization because I wouldn't be able to work through the process with him at that time.

With the new facility ready, the staff in place, and new clients in need, it seemed that Wellspring Living was just beginning to spread its wings. I had spent the previous nine months preparing for the call that had the news that we could serve our first girl. God had opened amazing doors through so many people, and as far as I knew, this new program would be one of the first of its kind in the country.

But now, I had to let it go. I had to let go of the opportunity to launch the program, to celebrate and support the staff, to meet our first girl. I was dedicated to these girls, but I was committed to my husband to care for him in sickness and in health. I wasn't sure what the future held for Dick or for the program, but I knew I could not leave his side. So I left the program in the capable hands of the Wellspring staff, turned off my phone, and committed myself to Dick's medical care.

For the next four months, I didn't even go on the campus where our staff worked diligently on this new aspect of Wellspring Living's mission. I didn't connect to hear how things were going. I felt that I needed to keep these thoughts and dreams out of my mind to be able to focus on my husband's care. So while I was at the hospital, God worked through this enthusiastic and dedicated staff to begin a groundbreaking program for traumatized young girls.

Miraculously, Dick's treatments went better than expected. Within ninety days of diagnosis, he was scheduled for a bone marrow transplant. I thought we were home free. I didn't know that the bone marrow transplant would be exponentially worse than the chemotherapy treatments. I saw my strong man lose sixty-five pounds in less than two months. Trips back and forth to Emory University Hospital for blood transfusions and overnight stays became part of our routine.

Then Dick's recovery shifted to home care. Apparently, something in my DNA makes me shriek when I witness medical procedures, so you can only imagine my shock when I realized I'd have to perform the cringe-worthy tasks of flushing Dick's port and changing his tubes. Many prayers and much grace saw me through those events. Many days were uncertain, yet it was evident that God had everything under control—the program, Dick's leukemia, and my poor nursing skills! How precious it was to learn firsthand that God was big enough to handle all these challenges and more.

Back to Work–God's Work

Little by little, after four months of Dick's hospitalization and treatment, I reintegrated myself into work with the girls while continuing to be a caregiver for my husband. Through this uncertain time, I felt God's assurance that Wellspring Living was His program, not mine, and that He did not rely on me to continue to do His work through it. And when I returned to Wellspring, I was so blessed to see how the ministry had grown!

On one of my first days back I had the opportunity to work with one of the girls, Amber, who had serious learning disabilities. State officials told us it would be next to impossible for her to complete high school requirements or get her GED. With my background as a teacher, I felt confident on this Tuesday morning that if I could spend time with Amber each week, I could teach her to read and comprehend her work.

Yet after one hour of working with her, I was totally frustrated and overwhelmed. In all my years of working with children with ADD and ADHD, I had never seen a case so severe. I remember going home that day and telling Dick about my frustration. His comment was, "Didn't you realize it would be hard?"

"Of course I did," I said. "But helping her is harder than I could have ever imagined."

In my prayers that evening for this beautiful, dark-haired girl, I told God that Amber might be too hard for us. Was this whole issue too difficult for God? Even with all the miracles I'd seen, I felt at that moment that this obstacle was insurmountable.

It was only two days later when I opened up my email and saw a surprising message:

You don't know me, but my best friend is in your women's program, and I am the director of Brain Balance [a holistic program for children with neurobehavioral and learning difficulties] at a location near your girls program. I wanted to reach out to you and offer our services if you have one girl who might have a difficult array of learning disabilities.

I was thrilled and relieved; help could not have come to us at a better time. By the time Amber completed the program, she was reading like crazy. At her Wellspring graduation ceremony, I remember smiling to see Amber sitting in her pretty dress, her head stuck in a book.

I was humbled and was reminded that obstacles are nothing to God. Amber was thriving, and so was my husband.

If You Change Your Mind

Tricia is one of our girls who knows all about obstacles—she's been knocked down enough times to qualify as a prizefighter. We feared that those obstacles would prevent us from helping her, but we didn't give up, and neither did she. Here is part of Tricia's story, in her own words.

For as long as I can remember, my mom was an alcoholic. My home was always filled with drugs, drinking, and a thick fog of smoke. It was during those early years of chaos that family members first molested me. Luckily, when I began elementary school, I had a temporary escape from the chaos. That all changed when I entered high school. I just didn't fit in, so I left school and eventually left home. I was determined to overcome the mountains that faced me, whatever it took. I got a job at the Dairy Queen at the age of fourteen by lying about my age, but I was still a homeless teenager. I felt I had to make my own way, but the reality was that I was vulnerable to anyone who would provide for me.

That's when Jim entered my life. I thought this man would be my ticket to "normal." But his idea of "normal" involved sex and drugs, and it wasn't long before he drugged me, launching what would become an addiction in my life, and I got pregnant. My life began to spiral out of control. In just a few short years, I had become trapped in a situation that felt uncomfortably close to my environment I longed to escape as a child. Two children later, the violent threat of people around us [remained], but I couldn't navigate myself and my kids out of this toxic situation all on my own.

One day the inevitable happened: I lost custody of my girls. My heart had been ripped out, but I couldn't see a way to change my situation. I remained chained to Jim, who I thought loved me when in fact I was just a commodity used for his pleasure and those he forced me to serve. It took me a long time to admit that he was my pimp. For almost five years, he kept me high on drugs, living in hotels, servicing his clients. The relationship was so physically and mentally abusive that I couldn't tell which way was up anymore. I remember days when he locked me in a dark bathroom because I hadn't made enough money for him that day. I was terrified, feeling like I was suffocating. To this day, I am afraid of the dark.

One night in fall 2009, Jim had me working out on the streets. Out of the dark, the police picked me up. And they were not only the police, but also producers from a new CBS television program called *Street Intervention*. They offered me a thousand dollars if I would consider participating in their show for the next twenty-four hours. It would include staying in a nice hotel, with good meals, spa treatments, and meeting someone who could help me. It sounded like a dream—so I agreed.

As twenty-four hours came to a close, they took me back to the dirty street where they had picked me up, where I met Mary Frances and another girl from Wellspring. They asked if I wanted to leave this life.

But I was so entrenched in my ways, so ready to give up on myself like everyone else in my life had, that I didn't see a way out even when offered one. I screamed "No!", took the money, and left.

Life continued in this vicious circle for the next nine months until I was arrested and sent to jail, where what should have been a huge obstacle turned out to be a lifesaver. I was in a residential substance abuse treatment program while in jail. My counselors observed my determination to overcome my obstacles and helped me turn my life around. In the spring, I was nearing graduation, and my counselor asked if I knew of a place where I could continue getting back on my feet. Even though it had been a couple of years, I vividly remembered the night those two women tried to help me, and even one's name had stuck with me—Mary Frances. My counselor agreed to help, but also cautioned me not to get my hopes up in case we couldn't find Mary Frances or Wellspring Living would not have an open spot for me.

But we did find contact information for Mary Frances, and I wrote her a letter asking if I could get into the program. My counselor spoke with their assessment director, and Wellspring said yes! Everything was planned for me to go into Wellspring Living in May, but then I got very sick. I found out that I had cancer, and that it was potentially fatal. My counselors responded to my needs, and I saw wonderful doctors who worked with me through several months of chemotherapy, internal and external radiation, and several blood transfusions. Finally, in September, I completed my treatments. I was strong enough to enter the program in November.

I had survived my bout with cancer, I was out of my former lifestyle and in a recovery program, and my kids entered the care and custody of my family, enabling me to see them again. Everything seemed like it was going well—until my third week in the program. Wellspring got word from my probation officer that I had to appear in drug court. We arrived on the first Friday in December, and the first thing they did was run a drug test. Because I was still on chemotherapy for the cancer, my drug test came back positive. We tried to tell them it was a result of my chemotherapy, but no one would listen. They locked me up. Here I was, for the first time in my life, trying to live the right way, and no one would believe me.

The staff at Wellspring advocated on my behalf with letters and phone calls, and finally Mary Frances called the district attorney. On Christmas Eve, Mary Frances and her husband picked me up so I could spend the Christmas holiday with them.

I have faced many obstacles in my life, some not by choice and some as a result of my own poor decisions. But God has helped me to keep going so that I can now know Him and have a new life. And now that He is rebuilding my life, I am able to rebuild my relationship with my girls.

The Night We First Met Tricia

I recall meeting with Tricia that Saturday night when the CBS crew returned her to the track, the Atlanta thoroughfare where johns (the "customers" in sex trafficking) go to find girls and pimps. Ashley, one of our graduates, had come with me. I was sure that if Ashley shared her new life of hope, Tricia would choose to enter the program. We pleaded with Tricia to choose a new way to live. I just couldn't believe it when she refused and stormed off.

Ashley and I called after Tricia as she walked away, but she kept moving, her back turned away from us. But I decided I wasn't going to let this opportunity go to waste without giving it all I had. I rushed after Tricia, reached out, and handed her my card. "If you change your mind," I said, "please call me." Tricia walked on.

There I stood at 11 p.m. on a dangerous street in Atlanta, in total disbelief and, quite frankly, mad. Selfishly, I couldn't believe that I had spent so much time with this girl, and she still rejected my offer. What a waste of time for my husband and Ashley, for Ashley's husband and her children.

Tricia didn't call the next day or the next week or the next month or even the next year. But an impression was made that night, one that lingered in Tricia's mind for the next couple of years. It was April 2011 when I received Tricia's letter, and shortly after that, a phone call. She was finally ready to take on the obstacle of changing her life. As I thought back, I was humbled to think of my self-centered attitude a few years before, and so glad that we'd invested the time to offer Tricia a chance.

We never know how long change will take or what roadblocks we'll face, but God does. Sometimes it seems that our efforts are wasted, that what we're attempting is beyond us. But when God is on our team, we have unlimited power.

Jesus once said, "What is impossible with men is possible with God" (Luke 18:27). At Wellspring, we've seen many obstacles that look impossible to overcome, but we also get a front-row seat to watch Christ make a way.

13~ We Become Her Community

When it comes to a woman in trouble, whether it's because of addiction, abuse, or other harmful life situations, the community that surrounds her is equally as important as her choices. Beginning in middle school, parents are usually removed from the primary seat of influence in a young person's life, and peers move in. During this time, frightened parents who truly desire what's best for their child must watch as they are replaced by those who are generally as self-centered and reckless as their own teen. It is critical, then, for a loving community to recognize when the teen is being harmfully influenced, and to pull her back from the road to destruction.

Sometimes the need for community is so great that Wellspring will open its doors to women who may not have walked the specific road of sexual abuse or trafficking. Stacy came to us after many years of meth addiction, partying, and drinking.[26] She had a loving family that wanted the best for her, but they had no idea what to do or how to help her. On the inside, she felt broken. It has been said that children are great observers but poor interpreters. Somehow Stacy saw herself as less loved by her family than her other siblings, particularly by her dad. Even though her dad never intended to communicate this feeling, she felt unimportant to him.

Throughout middle and high school, Stacy never felt like part of the "in" crowd. Although she was a cheerleader, Stacy wasn't popular and felt like an outsider. It was difficult for her to make close female friends. But boys were another matter. When Stacy was with a group of guys she lovingly referred to as "the boys," she felt accepted and safe to be herself. Then Stacy found acceptance in another group—the potheads and meth users. They loved and accepted her too, and having found a way to escape ongoing feelings of rejection and to finally be "in," Stacy started down a dangerous road.

That road was a six-year cycle of using methamphetamine, driving under the influence, and other high-risk behaviors, which increased the emotional distance between Stacy and her family. Stacy started showing up high to important family events or missed them altogether. Whenever she didn't show, her family wondered if Stacy was even alive. When she did show up, they questioned how long she'd live.

The party life was all around Stacy. Her days and nights were filled with people and excitement. Yet she still went to bed every night with her constant companions—loneliness, emptiness, and despair—which led her right back to meth to escape them.

When Stacy's family and friends had run out of options, they bravely and wisely decided to hold an intervention. They were determined to change the situation, and to never stop trying. Her parents called everyone they knew who loved Stacy to their house one day. One by one they expressed their fears, concern, and most importantly, love for Stacy. There were ex-boyfriends, uncles, aunts, friends, and the whole family.

More than being just caught off guard, Stacy was furious. She didn't realize that this was just what she needed. She didn't throw herself into the arms of her family and thank them for wanting to change the course of her life and save her from herself. No, Stacy sat there silently, growing more livid with each person's comments.

Recovery is always in the context of relationships, people who love us enough to put up with denial, relapse, and dumb decisions.

Her thoughts and words were all denials: *I'm not an addict. Interventions are for addicts! I don't have a drug problem. I could stop if I wanted to. I choose to live this way. I enjoy my life! Why can't they understand that?*

Soon Stacy stood up and stormed out of the house. Her family had no idea if they would ever see her again.

Two days later Stacy came to Wellspring Living, saying she would stay for only a few days to please her family. Stacy was still angry about the intervention and still in denial about her need for life change. But over the next two weeks she settled in, applied for the long-term program, and began her journey to healing.

Stacy had one of the strongest family support systems of any of the women we've served, and they made a huge difference in her recovery. No one recovers from addiction in isolation. Recovery is always in the context of relationships, people who love us enough to put up with denial, relapse, and dumb decisions. This perfectly describes Stacy's family, despite her view of them. They called and visited as often as possible. They never let Stacy get discouraged and wouldn't let her quit. Little did they know how much the whole family would change as a result of her recovery.

Even though her parents had divorced, the two of them, along with Stacy's stepfather, served as a trio of support. Stacy's younger sister was also very ready to have her sister back—Stacy had missed so much of her young life. Forgiveness and love constantly poured out of the four of them and filled the holes Stacy had been looking to mend with meth.

Then everyone signed up for family therapy. Stacy's father, Don, was the first to participate. He was a serious, no-nonsense business-man. Stacy was nervous about the first session, unsure how it would go. She expected her father to come in and be his usual self—strong, firm, emotionally detached, and matter-of-fact. But we were all amazed at what happened.

Don arrived right on time to the appointment with his business "game face" on. I began to ask simple questions about how he felt regarding where Stacy was and his hopes for her future. In the past, Stacy had always experienced lectures from her father and felt con-demned by him. We were both shocked when Don choked up and the tears began to flow.

Don wiped his face with a handkerchief, turned to his daughter, and looked her squarely in the eyes. "Stacy," he said, "I know this isn't all your doing. A lot of this is my fault. I should have been more clued in to what you were going through. I . . . I want to do whatever it takes to help you heal and get well."

After all those years of trying to find love in all the wrong places, Stacy realized that she was loved beyond words. This session became a turning point for her, and also a transformative catalyst for her whole family. Stacy's mom also came for family sessions and learned how to rebuild life with her daughter. Her sister came and reconnected with her once-lost sibling. Stacy finally realized what her mother, father, step-father, and sister had known all along—that she was worth the effort.

It wasn't long before Stacy and her dad started having father-daughter dates and getting to know each other on a new level. When he spoke at Stacy's graduation, there was scarcely a dry eye in the room. He told the story of regaining his beautiful daughter and how his life had been transformed as a result of her recovery. This was not just the transformation of a young woman, but also the evolution of an entire family and her community rallying around her.

A Friendship Restored

Childhood sexual abuse has a toxic ripple effect, not just in a young girl's life, but also in her entire community, her family, and her friends. Many times we assume that when a young woman can't get life to work, the problem is all about her. The reality, however, is that if one family member has a problem, healing is needed throughout the family. As humans, we are undeniably interconnected. We need each other to survive and thrive. The concept of community is that we all rely on one another for healthy living, so a girl's family and friends are affected by the destruction she experiences, and can also play a significant part in helping her to recover.

Brittany and Becky are two friends who know the power of community. They grew up in similar families, with great parents and a comfortable lifestyle, but their lives began to diverge when Brittany became a wife and mother and Becky found herself in a vicious cycle of addiction. Listen to Brittany tell their story.

Becky and I became best friends at a Christian school when we were thirteen. From that point on, we were inseparable. We roomed together at college and served as maid of honor in each other's weddings. Our husbands were even best friends.

After both of us were married and starting to have kids, I noticed for the first time that Becky was not just a social drinker. She and her husband had moved to Florida, and I knew Becky was miserable in her new "home." When I called her during the day, I could tell she'd been drinking. I became increasingly worried and asked her to please stay home and not drive anywhere. But every day that we talked, I heard the same relaxed slur in her voice. It was impossible for us to have the normal conversations that sustained our twenty-year friendship because her mind was elsewhere almost every time we spoke.

When our families decided to take a vacation together to the beach in the summer of 2005, I looked forward to reconnecting with my old friend, and perhaps seeing a change in her. The trip turned out to be a complete disaster. Who was this person? Becky was emotionally almost unrecognizable. She was drunk or hungover the entire time. We fought because I was hurt, angry, and confused. I just wanted my friend back. It took seeing Becky in person to realize that things were about to change in a big way. This person who was closer than a sister to me was now someone I did not enjoy being around. My heart was broken for her, and even though she stood right in front of me, I missed her. For a few painful months, we didn't even talk to each other. We both felt confused about this foreign distance between us, and more importantly, why we couldn't seem to fix it.

But then I thought about how I would want a good friend to treat me if I were in her shoes. I was determined to be supportive of Becky, but I had no idea what needed to be done. Becky knew she was in trouble too. She went to a few rehab centers in her hometown, but ultimately she needed Jesus. We both needed Jesus. I was not where I needed to be spiritually either.

I knew about Wellspring Living because of my mom, who was on the founding board of directors, and so did Becky. Mom had watched countless lives change as a result of Wellspring. She was always talking about the girls and the program at family gatherings, so we were very familiar with its work, but neither of us dreamed that Wellspring was going to save not only our relationship, but also the life of one of us.

My mom kept telling me that Becky needed Wellspring, but I knew Becky was not going to like the suggestion of being away from her kids for any period of time—I wouldn't have either. My mom invited Becky to come to Wellspring and try it for herself, and Becky wasn't interested.

[A little later] her addiction took a turn for the worse. Becky had convinced herself for a long time that her drinking only affected herself, when in reality it was causing her marriage and family to deteriorate. "Continued failure to maintain sobriety led Becky to face the bitter reality that she could not conquer her addiction alone. Becky took a bold step and entered Wellspring, even though it meant separation from her husband and children for several months."

While Becky was in the program, I began going with my mom and another board member to take the girls out to dinner. The two of them had started a tradition of treating the girls out to nice restaurants, places they would never go on their own, once a month. They wanted to let girls be girls! So, once a month, classes let out early to let the girls do their hair and makeup and prepare for a girls' night out, and I went with them. Over candlelit dinners and riverside picnics, these girls who I had heard about for so many years suddenly came to life for me. I realized they were girls just like me. In fact, a few wrong turns and I could have easily been a Wellspring girl myself.

I visited Becky every Sunday afternoon, and the slur in her voice and the cloud in her eyes disappeared. I had my best friend back— and not only that, but I gained many new friends who I met in the home, and remain friends with to this day. I love to brag on these amazing young women—whose determination and devotion endlessly inspire me.

I realize now that nothing was going to change until we both realized that only Jesus could repair our broken relationship. Only constant prayer could have so miraculously mended our friendship. Today, I am so proud of who Becky has become. I may have once been frustrated with her on the phone, but now I call her for spiritual advice. Her walk with the Lord is awesome!

Abuse and its repercussions threaten not only the survivor of the abuse but also every one of her relationships. However, as Brittany and Becky demonstrated, equal measures of patience, love, and courage, combined with a reliance on the Lord, can overcome both the obstacles to a survivor's healing and her most cherished relationships.

Joining Forces with Organizations

The beast that is sex trafficking has many tentacles, so we connect to as many varied organizational partners as possible in our efforts to address the wide array of needs in battling sex trafficking and helping survivors. These partners may train law enforcement officials on how to work with our girls, attack the problem of demand for trafficked women, explore prevention methods, promote community education, or offer aftercare to Wellspring graduates.

Three of these organizations recently came together to send a message to our state legislature that the children of Georgia needed their help. It all started in 2001 with Kaffie McCullough, a community activist who became instrumental in assisting law enforcement agencies and courts address the needs of young victims of trafficking. Kaffie is the campaign director of "A Future. Not a Past," a project of youthSpark, a nonprofit organization dedicated to "Ignite Justice. Inspire Change" for at-risk youth.

I first talked with Kaffie when Wellspring was just beginning the girls program. (My husband was undergoing his leukemia treatment, and I had plenty of time to think and pray while I cared for my husband's needs in that hospital room.) I was inspired by her tenacity. Kaffie and others expressed the need for state legislators to pass new laws in Georgia that would protect children, provide care for victims, and prosecute offenders. During the annual Lobby Day at the state capitol, those against child sex trafficking and exploitation lobbied for legislative action. Back home with my ailing husband, I cheered their efforts.

During slow times at the hospital, I read a historical book describing the White Rose Society, a youth movement against Hitler's regime. As I read, I realized what a perfect, tangible symbol this could be for our girls.

We would give every legislator a white rose, along with a letter asking them to protect the innocence of our children.

I shared my idea with Kaffie, and then we put our heads together with another friend, Cheryl DeLuca-Johnson, who is the executive director of another organization fighting sex trafficking called Street GRACE. Together, we launched a plan: armed with three hundred white roses, we would give one to every legislator along with a letter asking them to protect the innocence of our children and provide for those whose innocence was stolen as a result of sex trafficking.

It was a beginning. This initial effort by three organizations, and a multitude of volunteers, became known as an annual event called We Urge You. Today it attracts over eight hundred advocates each

February at the state capitol to send the clear message that we must end the sexual exploitation of our children.

Surprising Partnerships

Sometimes our partnerships arise out of unlikely places. In August 2010, I received a call from Jim Reese, president and chief executive officer of Atlanta Mission. This organization works diligently with the homeless population in our city. As one who loves his home, Jim, along with the Atlanta Mission board, was disturbed to learn that Atlanta was among the top cities for commercial sexually exploited children (CSEC). Jim called the state director of the Georgia Care Connection, who leads the state response to CSEC, and said, "We want to be a part of the solution, but we don't know how to work with victims. Who could we partner with to help out with this deplorable situation?"

The state director pointed Jim to Wellspring Living. As I sat in Jim's office, I was apprehensive about another partnership and expansion. I felt I couldn't keep up with what Wellspring Living was doing already. But I listened. By the end of the conversation, we were both convinced that God wanted us to work together.

It turned out that Atlanta Mission had two unused buildings with available efficiency apartments. One of the greatest needs for the girls we serve is a "step-out" service, a place to live and continue education once they leave our program. Going back to the community where they were exploited is usually not the best option. This seemed to be a new location for them to begin anew.

To be sure that this new idea was a good fit for both of us, we connected with the Urban Institute of Atlanta, which took on a "due diligence" study to determine the best use of the property. Over the next eighteen months, the staffs of Atlanta Mission and Wellspring Living spent time getting to know each other and dreaming together. A plan was created, a memorandum of understanding was signed, and the work began. It wasn't long before church groups stepped up to join us in the renovating process and to give financially toward the partnership.

The support we receive from churches is central to so much of what we are able to accomplish. In the fall of 2011, I received a call from a local church asking about our greatest need. I shared with them that we wanted to renovate those apartments for the girls in their next level of care after graduation. Right before Christmas, I was blown away by a generous gift that helped us begin the renovation of the apartments. As a part of their generosity campaign, partners actually set aside three workdays with activities that would engage their members in the project.

The first Saturday workday was my responsibility, so I planned more than enough work to do from 9 a.m. to 1 p.m. for twenty people. To my surprise, however, we had almost forty people, and by 11 a.m. they had completed everything on my long list and then some! The next two Saturdays, the same thing happened. I always had more than double the

Collaborating in the best interest of the sex trafficking survivors sends a new message: her new community is different, and this new community recognizes her value.

volunteers I anticipated show up, who then completed more than we planned. More than three hundred volunteers participated in completing the project in just two months, and this power boost also inspired other churches to get involved.

As of this writing, we are poised to move girls into the first building that has been retrofitted for their needs, and it won't be long before the second building is ready. By working together with many groups and individuals, both Atlanta Mission and Wellspring Living will benefit not only the girls Wellspring Living serves, but also many of the women that Atlanta Mission serves.

As Psalm 133:1–3 says about unity: "How good and pleasant it is when God's people live together in unity! It is like precious oil poured on the head, running down on the beard, running down on Aaron's beard, down on the collar of his robes. It is as if the dew of Hermon were falling on Mount Zion. For there the Lord bestows his blessing, even life forevermore."

It is through the efforts of families, friends, and partnerships like these that we change our girls' expectations of the future and give them hope. Survivors of sexual exploitation have already experienced the failures of individuals, organizations, and agencies at the time of their greatest need. But collaborating in the best interest of sex trafficking survivors sends a new message to a girl: her new community is different, and this new community recognizes her value. It shows her that while people of her past may have used her, this new community exists to serve her.

When people rally together to support a good cause, it shouts a second message to the community at large, that people can work unselfishly together if our eyes are on God and on those in need, rather than on our own advancement. I believe this is the way God meant for us to work. When we allow God to lead, what a refreshing message is communicated!

14~ We Can Be Creative

Many people want to join the fight against sex trafficking but don't know how to help. Andy Brophy is one person who found a creative way to make a difference while drawing others to the cause. This is his story.

Andy Brophy ran his finger across the soft green velvet of the pool table before framing his next shot. He was in the spacious basement of an upscale home, taking senior portraits of a soon-to-be high school graduate. The house was impressive—two stories plus the basement, set on an Atlanta golf course in a country club neighborhood.

A few minutes later, the future graduate's father walked in. Steve wore a white, short-sleeve, button-down shirt and dark slacks. His handshake was firm, typical of a CEO, which was exactly what Steve was. The red Corvette in the driveway completed the picture in more ways than one. It was a great prop for a photo of his son about to take on the world after a successful high school career.

Two months later, photographer Andy found himself in a very different room in a very different neighborhood. The space was only eight-by-ten feet, lit by a single dim bulb dangling from the concrete ceiling. A corner fan battled the heat with little success. The room was divided by a curtain. On Andy's side of the room stood a petite woman in her late twenties. She had long, dark hair that was tied up on her head, and she wore layers of wraps in several colors. On the other side of the room, Andy saw a simple bed. In the shadow, a man sat on the mattress, waiting.

Andy was in a brothel in India, taking photos for As Our Own, an organization dedicated to rescuing children in India from exploitation and providing them with lifelong care. It was day one of the trip. Andy knew he was a world away from the beautiful Atlanta home of just a few weeks before.

As members of the As Our Own team spoke with the woman, Andy watched her and tried to convey his compassion with a smile. She didn't return it. Her expression was distant, as if she were looking through the visitors. *She's not completely there,* Andy thought. *Part of her has been taken.*

The reality of the moment stunned Andy. It was lunchtime, yet business at the brothel was in full swing. Lines of men snaked through the narrow streets and alleys. Women, and sometimes girls, hustled to meet their customers' expectations.

After more than a week in India, Andy felt rocked to the core. What he'd seen was a tragedy. How could people live this way? How could they do this to each other? Wasn't anyone outraged that these women were being treated like cattle or worse? He'd heard of sex trafficking before, but this was the first time he'd seen it up close.

As a photographer, he had work to do, and Andy kept his emotions in check throughout the trip so he could stay focused behind the lens. On the bus ride to the airport for the flight home, however, the dam finally burst. He dropped his head and began to cry.

Back home in Atlanta, Andy was happy to be reunited with his wife, Jenica, and their six-month-old son. Yet it wasn't long before

Jenica revealed shocking news. Did he remember the senior portraits he took near that golf course a few weeks before? The father, Steve, had been arrested for child molestation. He had reportedly paid $600

Andy had just traveled to a destitute region halfway around the globe to help an organization fight sex trafficking, and now he was finding it in his own backyard.

to a pimp to have sex with a twelve-year-old girl at a Days Inn motel.

Andy tried to wrap his mind around this. Not long ago, he'd met this man. He'd been in his comfortable home and shaken his hand. Andy had just traveled to a destitute region halfway around the globe to help an organization fight sex trafficking, and now he was finding it in his own backyard. It put a face to both sides of the coin—the perpetrators, and the women and girls who were ensnared by them, in corners of the world both affluent and impoverished. Suddenly the sex industry was very human, and very real.

Now all Andy had to figure out was what to do about it.

Combining Passions

Andy grew up outside of Peoria, Illinois, where he committed his life to Christ at age ten and earned a degree in youth ministry and adolescent studies from Judson University. After graduating, he took a job at an Atlanta church as its outreach director.

As Andy ministered to Atlanta youth, he heard whispers about the high level of sex trafficking in the city (many reports place Atlanta among the top three cities for sex trafficking in America). He urged teens to be aware of it and to get involved in fighting it. Some did, joining programs that raised awareness and even writing letters to girls who were attempting to put their trafficking past behind them and start new lives.

Andy's passion for Jesus and for ministering to young people soon extended to a third interest: photography. He picked up his first camera in 2008 and found he had a gift for capturing stirring images. The deeper he dove into the world of photography, the more convinced he became that it should be his full-time vocation. In September 2010, at the age of twenty-six, he launched a freelance photography business.

Starting a new career didn't diminish Andy's desire to minister and serve, however. When he was invited to go on the November 2010 India trip by As Our Own, he quickly accepted. Now, Andy was sure his back-to-back encounters with the world of sex trafficking were no coincidence. He felt that the Lord was up to something and that he needed to respond.

"I want my photography to have a tangible ministry," Andy told Jenica. "So how can I use what I'm shooting here at home for restoration like I did for As Our Own?" The question gnawed at him.

It was at an art show featuring the images from the India trip that Andy met two young women from the Wellspring Living staff, Merridith Thomas and Dana Konick, and discussed an idea to host a musical event that would raise funds to battle sex trafficking. He was enthusiastic about the idea, yet Andy felt there was still something more he should do.

Andy thought about his primary photography business: weddings. *I see the wedding day as a celebration of love, commitment, and beauty. These two people are committing themselves to each other in an act of selfless love. When you look at trafficking, you have someone exploiting another person, stealing their love, stealing their beauty, in an act of selfishness. They're abusing another person to try to get something for themselves.*

Andy sat up. *Man*, he thought. *What a powerful statement it would be if wedding couples, brides and grooms, chose to use this one day to not*

only celebrate their love and new life together but also raise awareness of
what's going on in the city with trafficking. How cool would that be?

The more Andy considered it and discussed it with Jenica and others, the more certain he was that this was the path he needed to take. But what would they call it?

One evening, Andy sat down with his wife at their kitchen table to brainstorm. In front of him was a notebook filled with wedding words: *ring, dress, flowers, love,* and many more. One suggestion, With This Ring, seemed promising but was discarded when Andy realized that a number of wedding-related companies had the same name.

"I think the concept here is sacrificial love," Andy said. "Something along those lines."

"Give away love . . . love giveaway," Jenica said.

"Right, like that, only less corny."

They sat in silence a moment, brows furrowed.

"What about 'love gives way'?" Jenica said.

Andy smiled. He wrote it down. He said it aloud: " 'Love gives way.' Yeah, that could work."

Soon they had a concept that went with the name and what they hoped to achieve—brides and grooms choosing that their love gives way to the recovery and restoration of exploited girls.

The idea took shape. Andy would offer each of his wedding clients the opportunity to participate in the Love Gives Way program (www. thewhiteumbrellacampaign.com/video/#Love). If they said yes, Andy would donate $500 of his photography fee to Wellspring Living. The bride and groom would also encourage their guests to give gifts to the girls in the program, in addition to giving gifts to the couple. The girls would even register their needs and wishes at local stores so wedding guests could buy them in the same manner that they would have for the engaged couple.

Andy was excited. It was coming together. He even knew the perfect couple to help launch the project.

A Perfect Start

Cindy Simmons is an on-air personality at radio station WSTR–FM (Star 94) in Atlanta. She met Andy in 2009 when he came to take photos of the radio station staff. They hit it off and stayed in touch. Cindy joked more than once that she wanted Andy to be her photographer when she got married someday.

In May 2011, Cindy and a friend attended the As Our Own art show featuring Andy's images from India. She left the event in tears. The photos and the story they told of trafficking overseas left a powerful impression.

Later that month, Cindy *did* get engaged. "I'm not kidding this time," Cindy said on the phone. "I really do want you to shoot our wedding."

"That's great," Andy said, "because my wife and I have been working on an idea, and this could be a perfect fit if you're on board."

Andy explained about the prevalence of sexual trafficking in Atlanta. Cindy was shocked. Like many people, she had believed it was primarily an overseas problem. Then Andy told her about Love Gives Way. As soon as she heard the concept, Cindy loved it. She had recently battled breast cancer and was feeling especially grateful to be alive and to have the opportunity to start a new life. She and Eric had already decided that they didn't need new towels or a new blender. They wanted to do something else for

> Cindy and Eric wanted to do something else with their wedding gifts, something with deeper meaning.

their wedding registry, something with deeper meaning.

"Yes!" she told Andy. "I'm in—100 percent in."

Cindy and Eric didn't stop there. They wanted to see Wellspring in action, so they set up a time to meet the staff and toured one of the homes while the girls were taking classes. Cindy was so moved by what she saw happening in these young women that she persuaded her colleagues at Star 94 to designate Wellspring as their recipient for a citywide fund-raising competition. She shared with friends, family, and radio listeners what she was doing with her wedding gifts, and watched as the packages arrived one by one at her home. Cindy was filled with joy to know that each one would go to help one of the girls.

On December 3, 2011, Cindy, Eric, and their guests gathered at a local community church for an intimate wedding ceremony. Cindy wore her mother's wedding dress, as well as a necklace designed by another Love Gives Way partner, Mickey Lynn, that represented the Wellspring girls. Andy captured it all from behind his camera, glad to see his idea come to life in such a vivid and beautiful way.

"It was great," Cindy said. "No one brought a gift to the wedding because they'd already sent something for the girls. For us, the focus was on our exchange of vows before God, not getting gifts for ourselves. It was a special way to show what we stand for."

It was a beautiful, memorable night—the perfect start for the Love Gives Way campaign (www.thewhiteumbrellacampaign.com/video/#Love).

Something Bigger Than Themselves

Nearly every couple Andy has approached about Love Gives Way has responded with enthusiasm.[27] Since Cindy and Eric's wedding, more than fifteen couples have participated. One bride even put the Love Gives Way logo on her debit card so that when people asked about it, she would have an excuse to talk about the program.

Another bride-to-be, Jennifer Phillips, had been a mentor in Atlanta's Big Brothers Big Sisters program for more than seven years. She knew of the high incidence of sex trafficking in Atlanta and was alarmed by it. Knowing that many young girls are impressionable and at risk to pimps and abusers, she attended meetings about ways to battle trafficking and used social media to raise awareness about this critical issue. When Jennifer needed a photographer for her wedding, a friend recommended Andy. She discovered the Love Gives Way program and knew he was the right choice.

"My wedding day was even more special because not only was my Little Sister in my wedding, but we also knew that every time we saw the flash of Andy's camera, we, together, were helping the young girls in Atlanta. One's wedding day is meant to be special anyway with the uniting of two people, but when you combine that with a talented photographer doing amazing things for such a great cause, there are no words for it."

Andy is regularly encouraged by the enthusiasm of these couples.

"Love Gives Way is nothing without the brides and grooms," he says. "My wife and I may have come up with the idea, but it's the couples who get fired up about it and are doing something tangible to change lives. I am humbled and tremendously thankful that there are people out there who want to use their wedding day for something bigger than themselves."

Andy hopes to expand the program to other photographer partners who will also offer a Love Gives Way wedding package. "I've found that so many people want to leverage their gifts and abilities to do something like this. They just don't always know how to do it. When they hear about what we're doing, they so often say, 'Man, I've been thinking about how I could do something like that for so long. How can I get on board?'"

Once Andy's photography idea had taken off, he decided to try serving the Wellspring girls by videotaping their journey. Shannon was one of our recent Wellspring graduates; she had grown up in Ohio and dated a boy who persuaded her to move with him to Atlanta. After they arrived, Shannon was lured into a life of drug use that led to sexual abuse and exploitation before she found healing through Wellspring. Andy was moved by her story, and wanted to capture it in film to share it with others through a video shoot.

Shannon nervously tucked her dark hair behind her ears and sat cross-legged on a stool as she told her story. She clutched her Bible and notes tightly as she spoke and choked up as she described being trapped in a terrible situation. Yet her expression changed dramatically before the camera when she related how the staff at Wellspring provided counseling, helped her finish her schooling, and gave her the opportunity to give back to other girls in the program after she graduated.

When the video shoot was over, the participants lingered a few minutes to talk. Andy was encouraged to share about his photography and the Love Gives Way program. When he finished, Shannon looked him in the eyes, any signs of nervousness gone, and said, "That is so cool. Thank you so much."

For Andy, those few words were all he needed to keep praying and working to change the lives of trafficked girls. One life had been restored. Many more were waiting for love to give way.

15~ Pray for Her

The apostle Paul tells us to pray all kinds of prayers, in all kinds of circumstances. I am immensely grateful for the amazing prayer warriors who cover God's precious work in the lives of the girls and women we serve. This chapter is dedicated to those who make prayer a priority in the work of Wellspring Living.

It can be difficult to know how to pray for someone when you may not have faith that her circumstances can change. Yet over the years I've repeatedly seen the power of prayer in the midst of trauma and tragedy. If it were not for the thousands of people who weekly lift up to God the girls we serve, I don't believe any of us could persevere in what we do. Prayer is the invisible strength that holds us up every day.

When Paul urged the people of Ephesus to put on the armor of God, he also wrote, "And pray in the Spirit on all occasions with all kinds of prayers and requests. With this in mind, be alert and always keep on praying for all the saints" (Ephesians 6:18). The community that supports Wellspring Living certainly employs all kinds of prayers and requests on our behalf.

Each week we send an email to over four thousand people who

have committed to praying for the girls and women of Wellspring. We list specific requests and pair them with Bible verses to help our supporters know how to pray. When I first started sharing our requests, I wondered if this was an effective means of encouraging prayer. Did people really have the heart to pause while clicking through their emails, and pray for a girl they had never met, and probably never would? Yet over the years, so many people have told me that they prayed over each request the minute they received it. We have seen miracles within hours of pushing the send button.

Beyond this army of supporters, God has blessed us with a second team of seventy-five men and women who devote extraordinary amounts of time to pray for everything that concerns the work of rescuing, restoring, and renewing our girls and women. We recently opened a new residential facility for our girls, and one day walking into the building prior to occupancy, I was surprised to hear voices. When I entered the room, I found four of our prayer warriors clustered together, bringing the girls who would inhabit these rooms before God. It's not unusual for me to wake up in the morning, check my email, and find that dedicated friends of Wellspring have been up during the night, praying. These emails will be filled with Scriptures that perfectly speak to a situation I may not have even been aware of.

God has given these friends the unique capacity to stand in the gap and intercede for those who cannot pray for themselves.

Persistent Prayer for One Person

I have also seen the incredible power of focused, persistent prayer by one individual for another. Miki, for example, was one of our dedicated volunteers as well as a board member. She traveled two hours each Wednesday to teach a class on topics of interest to the girls at the Wellspring Living home. Sometimes she taught from a book or Bible study; other times she decided to forego any curriculum to address the pressing needs and issues concerning the girls that week. Even though it was a long drive, she smiled all the way home.

Miki prayed for all the girls, but one in particular, Sherry, found a special place in her heart. Sherry was beautiful, a star student, and from all outward appearances, it would be difficult to sense the brokenness she carried around with her everywhere from a hurting family and childhood sexual abuse. She was so competent that it was difficult for her to let go of her pride to enter the program.

After Sherry graduated from Wellspring, she moved into Miki's community. Sherry missed her Wellspring support group, opening the door to a deeper connection with someone she already knew and trusted, someone who'd already invested in her. Sherry and Miki began to meet weekly to talk and pray. Miki dedicated additional time to pray on her own for the specific issues they'd discussed.

There were many ups and downs to Sherry's new independent life, but this consistent prayer built a stable foundation in Sherry's life that she had never experienced before. Sherry's time with Miki reinforced what she had learned at Wellspring, and gave her further practical guidance in living it out. Sherry was able to walk with confidence into a bright future, knowing that Miki was praying for her every step of the way.

Prayed Safely Home

Chloe is another of our Wellspring girls who would say she has been deeply influenced by prayer. But unlike Sherry, Chloe didn't know she was being prayed for until many years later. This is the story in Chloe's words:

I'm sure there were people everywhere praying for me, but the one person who prayed without ceasing is my mom, Olivia. It is surprising that she would pour out prayers for me, because by the time I went off to college, I had shut my family out of my life, especially my mom. I was so sure of myself and wanted so desperately to be on my own that I refused to see or talk to Mom for ten years while I was at the peak of my drug and alcohol addiction. I assumed that she had given up on me, but that was far from the truth.

About six months into the Wellspring program, I finally visited my mom. I didn't know what to expect, but nothing could have prepared me for what happened next. Mom showed me a list of Bible verses she had typed up, but these were not just Bible verses—my name was written all over them. She had inserted my name into each verse, claiming these precious promises of God just for me. My mom had prayed these verses for me every single day over our ten years apart, not knowing whether I was dead or alive.

I had learned at Wellspring that God's Word is powerful, but here it was, silently, patiently at work in my life for a decade. I was shocked. I never would have dreamed that my mom loved me so much, and that God loved me even more.

Now I realize that God had His hand on me during my addiction. I think there was a reason He protected me so many times when I should not have survived. I think there was a reason I cried out to God toward the end of my addiction. I didn't even know who I was crying out to or why, but now I recognize that my change of heart was an answer to the prayers of a faithful, loving mom who kept praying against all odds.

Knowing how long my mom waited for an answer and how hard it was for her in the midst of her daughter's absence has made my faith in God unshakeable. Because of my mother's faith, I know

God hears me even when He doesn't answer how or when I want Him to. I know because He heard the prayers of my mom, and I know He hears mine.

Emergency Prayer

It's a relief to know that I too can call on God when I need immediate help and realize that He's listening and ready to respond. And because the entire existence of sexual abuse and trafficking is a crisis, we offer up many emergency prayers on behalf of our girls, and take comfort in knowing that God hears us.

Jason, a teacher in the girls program, sounded the emergency prayer alarm one day during a difficult class period. At its inception, there had been no males working in the Wellspring Living Girls program, but when Jason applied for a teaching position in the program, we realized the value for the girls to have a healthy male role model with safe boundaries as part of the program. Jason's wife, Sophie, had also been working with us, and after interviewing many candidates, we knew he was the right one for the job. He is a daily example in the classroom of a man who serves and respects women, and his and Sophie's involvement together at Wellspring provide the women with a view of a healthy marriage.

But on this particular day in Jason's class, it seemed that Diana, one of the girls, was having a rough time. She had just found out, once again, that her mom was canceling her visit. Snapping her notebook shut, Diana declared that she wasn't going to do her schoolwork. Jason tried to encourage her, but she interrupted, "I hate you, Mr. Jason. And I am *not* doing this math."

"Diana," Jason said, "I know you're having a rough day, but I believe in you."

Diana stormed off as if she hadn't heard a word. Jason has heard a lot of ugly things come out of the mouths of these teenage girls, but never a personal attack like this. It stung to hear these acidic words from a student, but even more, he was worried about the pain that had caused them. Jason knew this outburst had nothing to do with him or math. Jason immediately reached out to his friends by tweeting, "Most of you know what I do. This girl just told me that she hates me. I know she really doesn't. She needs God to touch her right now. Please pray for her."

Jason reported that within thirty minutes, Diana came up to him and said, "Mr. Jason, I didn't mean what I said. Thank you for believing in me."

I know that God's answers to our petitions, including emergency prayers, are not always what we had sought. Sometimes He has purposes that we can't see or understand, but I have no doubt that He hears each request out of His great love for us.

A Prayer Warrior

For some friends of Wellspring, prayer is simply everything. It is a calling, a way of life. I admire these spiritual giants and appreciate them beyond measure.

One of these people, Martha Jeane Giglio, has a special place in my heart and in the hearts of our girls. She lived almost her entire life in Georgia, grew up in the church, and committed her life to Jesus as a teenager. At the age of twenty, she met her future husband at a church picnic. He wasn't a churchgoing man, but he became one after meeting Martha Jeane. It was an early sign of the strong influence she would have on many lives.

Martha Jeane was a devoted Christian and mother, raising both a son and daughter. She was known by those close to her for her service and her connection to God. "I always felt she had this giant pipeline to God because she was such a prayer warrior," says Gina Shaw, her daughter. "Whenever someone had a need in our church, a terminal illness, a child who was sick, she was all about praying for that person. That's who she was."

This was a woman who took her calling to pray seriously. She was on her knees every day talking to God about her brothers and sisters, her son and daughter, their future spouses, and later, Martha Jeane's grandchildren. She prayed continually for friends. She also prayed for blessing on her church and ministries she was close to.

One of these ministries was the Passion movement, directed by her son, pastor and author Louie Giglio, and his wife, Shelley, and dedicated to igniting a spiritual awakening on college campuses and around the world. Once, during a Passion Conference event in Texas attended by as many as thirty thousand students, a storm attacked the area. The grounds were flooded. More than one person was struck by lightning. Martha Jeane spent the entire night facedown on the floor, beseeching God to change the weather so the people would be safe and the conference could go on. The sun came out the next day.

Another time, Passion sponsored and planned a world tour that would take its message to thousands. Approval for many of the team's passports, however, had been delayed. The logistics planning team was in tears, as it appeared key members would be forced to stay behind. Martha Jeane wrote down the names of every person and every issue in a notebook and prayed fervently for each. Amazingly, the passports began coming through.

In 2007, when Martha Jeane was seventy-four, a friend of mine told her about the work we do and the women and girls we serve at Wellspring. Martha Jeane had to check it out for herself. I remember meeting her for the first time as she toured the women's facility. She had short blonde hair that looked like it had just been styled, blue eyes, and a ready smile. She was so humble. She said, "I don't know if I have much to give, but I would really love to teach a class."

From the beginning, the women were totally enamored with this precious, gentle lady. They looked forward to their time with her each Tuesday. Martha Jeane engaged these young women by teaching, often sharing a DVD featuring instruction by her son on themes such as hope, grace, and seeing God as our Father and Creator. Yet she also spent many minutes simply listening to the women share about their struggles.

Martha Jeane never came to teach without her prayer notebook. Her tradition for the end of each class was to sit by each woman and ask how she could pray for her. Sometimes she wrote down the prayer requests the women shared, but most often each woman wrote in the notebook herself the specific difficulty she was experiencing. The women experienced on another level how sweet and accepting Martha Jeane was. She not only took their requests but also asked the following week how God had helped them work through their difficulty. Martha Jeane developed a bond with these women. They each had confidence that whatever troubles she faced were also a concern and prayer priority for Martha Jeane.

Martha Jeane had lived with Parkinson's disease for years, but in 2008, her health began to drastically decline. She was moved to an assisted living facility and was unable to continue teaching her classes. But that didn't stop her from praying for our girls. We asked them to write down their prayer requests to mail to Martha Jeane. Even when she was in an assisted living facility, she kept her notebook and these letters with her and prayed over them many times a day. Martha Jeane grew so familiar with them that even when she was too weak to open her eyes, just touching a letter was enough to remind her of that girl's story and needs.

Tiffany was one of these girls Martha Jeane prayed for, although she was skeptical of prayer at first. She'd had a difficult journey through losing custody of her daughter and fighting to get her back. Tiffany resisted the idea that someone would make a difference for her. In her prayer letter, she wrote, "I don't really know if this will help. I don't know who you are or why you're praying for me. I don't really know if your prayers can come true."

That only inspired Martha Jeane to pray even more. Lying in bed in the assisted living facility, she closed her eyes and prayed, "Here I am again, Lord, praying for Tiffany. You know all about her and exactly what she needs, but I want to ask on her behalf and trust that You will meet every need perfectly. " She offered up Bible verses, asked for protection for Tiffany, and prayed for her daughter to be returned to her. "Lord, I believe You are healing her," Martha Jeane prayed, "and I also know that You are able to bring her through."

> What she needs most is a warrior to pray for her, someone to carry her to the throne when she is too weak to carry herself.

When Tiffany's Wellspring graduation ceremony arrived, Martha Jeane felt well enough to attend. Tiffany spotted Martha Jeane, rushed over, and engulfed her in a hug. Both women smiled and sobbed.

"Gina," Martha Jeane said to her daughter, "this is the girl who didn't want me to pray for her." Everyone laughed.

Whenever I saw Martha Jeane, even if it was only for a few minutes, she reminded me that she was praying for me too. This caring, amazing woman passed away in 2010. I miss her, and her prayers, terribly. Martha Jeane may have looked like a quiet, gentle lady at first meeting, but when she was on her knees—which was often—she was a fierce warrior.

It's difficult for many of our girls to pray for themselves in the midst of restoration from horrific circumstances. What each one needs most is a warrior to pray for her, someone to carry her to the throne when she is too weak to carry herself. Some of our prayer partners, like Martha Jeane, have the opportunity to meet our girls face-to-face, but it always astonishes me to think that most of our prayer partners never actually meet the women they pray for. They may never see the fruit of their effort, but they keep praying anyway. They take time out of their busy schedules to pause and pray. They influence others to pray. They drive over an hour to meet and unite in powerful intercession. They sacrifice hours of sleep to cry out on their behalf.

The gratification for these prayer warriors doesn't come from seeing or even knowing all the details. Their focus is on being part of the solution toward her recovery. Their faithfulness and joy in service inspires me every day.

16~Believe in Her

When a girl is in the middle of trauma or trying
to recover from it, it's difficult for her to believe her
future will be any different from or better than her
past. It's our job to believe in her and for her. So many
times, it seems everything is working against her, with
very little working in her favor. Often, I am totally overwhelmed by
her obstacles and realize the only way to overcome them is through
God's intervention and His people stepping up. When I focus only
on her trauma and present reality, I find myself paralyzed. Looking
beyond the trauma is essential. The following "snapshot" of Patty
reveals why it is so important for us to believe for her and in her.

Patty's Story

Imagine leaving behind everything familiar to you so you can
spend a season of your life diving into your past of sexual and physical abuse, while also battling a chemical addiction you use as a coping
skill. In this state, it seems impossible that I'll ever be whole again
or that I could ever be a productive member of society. My sense of
self-worth has been so beaten down and so bound by the shame of
my past. The person who took my innocence and betrayed my trust
now has a great life. He's achieved his dreams and has high status
in his career. Here I am, overwhelmed and stuck in this mess. While

attempting to numb my pain, so many unintended consequences have occurred:

- Pain so deep that it led to my addiction to drugs, alcohol, and painkillers
- Shoplifting to support my addiction
- Clouded processing, making abuse from anyone acceptable.
- Boundary lines so blurred that I often don't recognize when someone is a safe person
- Damaged relationships with my parents and friends.
- Multiple "car wrecks," with paranoia and confusion my constant companion
- Multiple DUIs and run-ins with law enforcement
- Unending self-sabotage

I feel hopeless. I am the one left broken and defeated. I don't have the emotional energy to tackle the obstacles. I know I want something different for my life, but everything seems so out of reach. The time has finally come to rectify my past mistakes and begin to mend broken relationships. But who in their right mind would believe in me and give me another chance?

The Challenges of a Second Chance

As I've worked with our girls at Wellspring, the most disturbing reality I've discovered is how difficult it is for anyone who has truly turned her life around to show the world that she will make a fresh start. Trying to get a job when your background shows no credible work experience is almost impossible. We spend so much time trying to convince an employer to take a chance on one of our girls. Of course, we can't guarantee that she will perform well. We can only say that we will be there to support both her and her employer as she steps into her new job.

Many times, we must also address criminal charges in her past. When she was in the midst of her trauma, there was no consideration of rectifying those charges, but now it is an essential part of building a new path. However, the financial penalties are huge, and if she doesn't have a job, it looks impossible.

Finally, what if she has children? Will she ever be trusted again to be a good mom and be able to keep her children? That's exactly what Jordan, a young mom in our program, wondered.

Jordan's Story

I've never felt so alone, abandoned, broken, sad, and exhausted. In the past three years I voluntarily entered four different recovery programs, became hospitalized nearly ten times due to alcohol poisoning or withdrawal, and moved so many times I can't count. I yearned for healing and help, yet felt as though I kept trying to open locked doors. Looking back at the times I got so drunk that I didn't know how I'd gotten back to my place the next morning, times I had no place to sleep, times I rode with complete strangers, I seemed even to myself like a lost cause. I wondered how anyone else could see any hope for me either.

Just when I thought I'd done everything that a mother could do wrong, I made a horrible mistake. I decided to drink while my two daughters were visiting me, after I'd put them to bed. The next thing I remembered was waking up in the hospital and being served a warrant for my arrest. I was told I'd been charged with "second degree contributing to the deprivation of a minor child"—two counts, because I was intoxicated while I was responsible for their care. I went directly from the hospital to jail for seven days.

I couldn't believe I was in jail! Of all people, how could I be in jail? Yet alone in my cell, at the absolute end of myself, I began to realize the gravity of my situation. If I truly loved my daughters as I said I did, why did I drink that way? I asked myself that question from the most sincere part of my heart. I believe God was whispering in my ear during those days. I spent the first thirty days after I got out of jail seeking help. But it was too late. No matter how hard I tried, the inevitable was rising like a dark storm—I would lose contact and visiting privileges with my little girls.

I felt grey when I came to Wellspring at the end of August 2011. I loved my daughters deeply, but the joy and color they brought into my life was drained from me. I had nightmares for weeks in which either my daughters didn't recognize me or else I wasn't allowed to see them at all. Many nights I woke up crying. I felt like my heart had a hole in it. Still, I knew something was calling me; maybe it was even God Himself.

> I felt like my heart had a hole in it. Still, I knew something was calling me. Maybe it was even God Himself.

No one else would help me now. Even my father had helped my husband file for divorce. I saw myself as an alcoholic who'd already failed at three recovery homes, a mother without her children, an embarrassing wife, a disappointing daughter, and now a legal offender in trouble. Who would invest in someone like that? I didn't say these things often or out loud, but I did think them when I laid my head on the pillow at night. Those nights of not having an answer, of not knowing where my future would take me and if it would include my daughters, were the absolute worst. They were worse than losing my husband and not getting a phone call from my family. My heart didn't call out for anything more deeply than my girls.

But God gave me hope through the staff and volunteers at Wellspring Living. He used them to open a tightly locked door for me. One September afternoon, an attorney named Jeff came to the assessment center. Wellspring had contacted Jeff to see if he could help me. It seemed that we talked for hours. I told him everything about my situation. I was so surprised. He didn't seem to judge me. He didn't look at me the way I assumed he would after I told him everything. No one that I knew of was making him do this for me. Yet he was helping me.

At that first meeting, he asked if he could pray for me. I have never known a man to be so open and hopeful that God would answer our prayers. It was a simple but powerful prayer that I still remember to this day: "Father God, we sit here before You now, asking You to direct us as we seek Your best for Jordan and her girls. We ask You for wisdom and favor." He spoke as if God were his best friend.

Jeff continued to work with me at Wellspring, spending hours going over paperwork and questions, even on a Friday night. Every time I saw him, we prayed together. I felt so comfortable in his presence and I knew, I just knew without a doubt, that the worst was over. My final divorce court date arrived, and Jeff told me to not worry, to take comfort in reading Job 42:2 and Psalm 46. I did read them, and I put my heart into God's hands. I asked that God would use my life for the good of my daughters. I had no control over the outcome of that day, and I couldn't have gotten through it without God and the people He put by my side through it all.

The divorce judge outlined step-by-step how, with improvements in my recovery, I could graduate to more time and involvement in my daughters' lives. What a blessing! As I sit here typing this, I can't help but cry tears of joy. I couldn't have imagined I would ever reach this point, and I'm not even halfway through the program!

Jeff tells a different side of the story. That fall afternoon when he first met Jordan, Jeff saw a distraught, terrified young woman who was drowning in her feelings of abandonment. Jordan couldn't afford a lawyer to represent her in the proceedings, but Jeff felt God prompting him to help her despite the financial and emotional cost.

"I'd always wanted to personally be involved in helping someone who had no resources," Jeff told us, "someone with no hope other than the intervention of God. I guess that was my chance to take a step of faith. To believe for Jordan meant I had to first believe God for the impossible, because from an attorney's point of view, we didn't have a chance!"

In Jeff's mind, two things stuck out from that first meeting. One was Jordan's love for her children, and the other was Jordan's surprise and gratitude that anyone would be willing to help her. After that first meeting, it became clear that her disbelief that anyone would help was a result of the lack of support from her immediate family, as well as a husband who wanted her gone, and a world around her telling her she would never make it. Later during their time in court, the opposing attorney asked pointedly, with no regard for the grief Jordan was experiencing, "Since you've been to programs before and failed every time, why should we believe this time around is going to be any different?"

While that may have been the first time anyone vocalized the question to Jordan, it was clearly a question in the minds of the people around her that played out in the way they treated her. It was also a question she wrestled with herself.

When others tell one of these precious women that she's a failure and she begins to believe it herself, this is the critical moment when we need to step in. Like Jeff did for Jordan, we must proclaim that we believe in her and in our God, who is able to do beyond what we can imagine. We believe that the Lord created her with a purpose and a destiny. We believe God began a work in her and that He will be faithful to complete it. We believe she will have the courage and the strength to persevere and endure when the suffering seems unbearable, because God is with her. And we believe in God's strength enough to support her with our words, time, and resources, asking nothing of her in return.

That's exactly what Jeff did. He continued to work for Jordan in spite of the overwhelming odds. By their next court appearance, the judge was miraculously sympathetic to her recovery process. He too believed that the future held something great for both Jordan and her children. She now has regular visitation with her daughters that will continue to increase as she completes phases of

> By their next court appearance, the judge was miraculously sympathetic to Jordan's recovery process.

her recovery. She presses forward, now believing that the day will soon come when she is fully reunited with her children and can continue to become an even healthier, more godly mother to them.

It's easy to hear the parable of the good Samaritan and comfort ourselves with the thought that if we were to encounter a wounded traveler on the side of the road, we would stop to help. But what about the young woman in recovery who needs but can't afford dental work? What about the girl whose mother never taught her how to buy groceries, manage finances, or even read a book? What about the mother who was never shown how to parent her children? Will we meet these women in their places of need, abandoned and bleeding on the side of the road? Will we take the time and expend the resources it will take to meet those needs? If we as a community of faith will not demonstrate true belief in the power of God to restore her, who will?

We must believe for her . . . and in her!

17~ Stand with Her

God continually amazes me with the staff He has gathered at Wellspring Living. They are passionate individuals who are willing to do whatever it takes, offer relentless support, and unconditionally love each of our girls. Amanda Johnson is no exception. She began as our lead teacher and is now the director of education for the girls program. Amanda eloquently expresses why we must stand with each girl.

by Amanda Johnson

When I returned from one year serving in South Africa, I couldn't get the images and faces of sex trafficking out of my mind. I had worked there in a group home with young girls who had escaped this predatory system, and it wasn't long before I grew to love each of them. They were beautiful, intelligent, and amazing young ladies, bursting with life and potential. It wrecked me to learn that they had been subjected to such abuse. How could anyone see these girls as objects to be used and then left for nothing? How could humans treat fellow human beings in such a heartless manner?

I had no idea how to be a part of the solution, but I felt a stirring in my heart. I wanted to stand for justice. I wanted to stand with each girl.

As I researched the issue further, I learned that Atlanta is a major hub of sex trafficking. I realized that God had brought me back to Atlanta to fight the cause in my own backyard. When I called different groups working on the issue, I discovered Wellspring Living. They called me back two days later to say they had a job opening in their new program for girls who had been trafficked. The more surprising part was that it was a teaching position. A teacher? I couldn't believe it! I'd taught school for the five years prior to my time in South Africa. I never dreamed that teaching would continue to be a part of this new journey I was on. God had orchestrated the perfect job for me, one that would combine my passion to work with trafficked girls and my skills and gifts as a teacher. I was so excited to have the opportunity to teach the girls who entered the Wellspring Living program.

Why I Stand with Her

It never crossed my mind that I wouldn't be able to have a high school diploma by the time I was eighteen. It wasn't something I had to dream about. And high school was a fun time for me. I played multiple sports, had good friends, cheered at football games, and dressed up and danced at prom. Those four years were some of the best of my life!

The girls I work with cannot say the same thing. These girls missed most, if not all, of their high school classes. When they did attend, much of their time was spent in in-school or out-of-school suspension. They most likely failed most of their courses, often sleeping through them. They appeared to not care at all. Why should they care about school when they had so much other junk going on?

The girls I teach had encountered problems such as helping the family get money for rent, food, and utilities. They were responsible for taking care of their younger siblings. They had been pimped out every night and often beaten. Our girls didn't play sports after school;

they worked the streets after school. Our girls didn't attend football games on Friday nights; they went to the nearest hotel with their pimp to endure unwanted sex with men.

School is where these girls rest, where they get away from all the chaos. School is a sanctuary, but it isn't where they actually learn.

Despite all of this and despite what I believed when I first started teaching these girls, getting a high school diploma is actually very important to them. I continue to be amazed at just how much each girl wants to succeed in school. Our girls want to receive As, they want to be on the right grade level, they want to go back to school with their peers and not be behind. They want to show their parents

They want to go to prom, play sports, attend football games, socialize in the hallways, have a locker, and just be normal.

they can do it, they want to be the first in their family to get their high school diploma. They want to go to prom, play sports, attend football games, socialize in the hallways, have a locker, and just be normal.

Lucy was one such girl who spent time at Wellspring. She loved being social! She had a boisterous personality and wanted to be involved in everything. She wished she could be a cheerleader and be in the popular crowd. Lucy often expressed how bummed she was that she had to go to school in the Wellspring home instead of "regular" school.

For those reasons, I hated that she had to be in our program too. I wanted to see her flourish, to be class president, to be captain of the cheerleading squad. I wanted to see her out laughing and playing with her classmates, not going through a program for those who have been abused in such a horrific way. For the time we had her, though, she was definitely the head of our social community. She worked hard in school and improved. Lucy had struggled with school, so this was actually a good place for her. We were proud of the progress she made with us and were happy to see her get back to a "normal" life upon completing our program.

Not everyone is like Lucy, though. The reality is that our girls usually don't get to experience all these wonderful high school landmarks. What can they do? They can catch up to proper grade level, they often can maintain a B or even A grade average, they can graduate from high school, and they can make their parents proud. These are the things I hope to help my girls do. These are the things I fight for. I stand beside each girl because she has the right to a good education just like everyone else. She has the right to make something out of her life. So I stand by her and walk with her.

How I Stand with Her

Even though my students are eager to do well in school and are so proud of their newfound success, it doesn't come easy for them. Going to school while working through your trauma is not easy. One hour the girls are learning about geometry, the next they are in a counseling session talking about their past. Then they are expected to jump back into the rest of the school day. Some days, this works out just fine. It's our routine, and they get used to it. Other days, they just need a break. They need to come in and sit with their heads down. They need to color, draw, do a word search, talk with a mentor, or just listen to some music.

Deidra was a girl who often struggled after counseling sessions. Her family wasn't always supportive and usually believed the worst in her. She usually felt like she could do nothing right for them. After one session of family therapy, Deidra came back to class deflated and upset.

"Hey, Deidra, glad to have you back!" I said. "Are you ready to get started on your algebra?"

"Algebra?" she said. "Why should I do that? My mom thinks I'm a going to flunk out of school anyway. She doesn't think I'll pass ninth grade. I'm quitting school."

I knew she was blowing off steam. "What?" I said. "I don't believe that. Quitting school is definitely not something I see you doing. You've already accomplished so much since you've been here. You work hard every day. I've seen the goals you've set for yourself. I think it's time to prove to yourself and your family that you aren't a failure in school."

Deidra's face brightened. "I guess. But I'm not going to go announcing it to my mom every time I see her. I know she won't care. I'm just going to do this for me. "

"She might come around eventually, Deidra. Why don't you spend some time writing a letter to your mom? Express the things that are really on your heart. Tell her how much you desire her to know the real you—that you actually do care about school and want to succeed. Maybe you'll have the chance to share those feelings with her in a session one day. If not, then you'll have at least done this for yourself. If you still need some time after that, let me know. Otherwise, I'm coming back to tackle that algebra with you."

In the beginning, it was hard for me to help the girls find the balance between needing time and getting back to their schoolwork. How do I know if a girl is just slacking and not wanting to accomplish her schoolwork? How do I keep her motivated to work toward her goals? How do I know if she just truly needs a break from everything?

The reality is she nearly always needs the break. I have to constantly remember that these girls have been through so much more than most of us will ever have to go through. They are constantly

> Sometimes supporting her means chatting about what's on her mind. Other times it's teaching her how to solve an algebra problem. Our consistent presence helps the most.

reminded of their past while going through therapy or groups, and they are constantly reminded that they aren't at home with their family and friends and regular, everyday comforts. They live in a foreign place with foreign people and are expected to accomplish school goals. I work every day helping them do just that . . . through all the turmoil and pain.

Each day, when I come into the classroom, I assess where each girl is. I note whether it looks like she's going to have a good day or a rough day. I do this multiple times a day because anything can change their course for the day. But I do this gladly. I want to be able to meet each girl wherever she is emotionally and spiritually at each moment of the day. I want to be a support to her as she walks through this mess.

Sometimes supporting a girl means chatting about what's on her mind. Other times it's teaching her how to solve an algebra problem or reading a story from literature to her. It's our consistent presence that helps the most. She wants to know that we are coming back the next day to help with the next math problem or give the next test. She wants to know we are there for her, that we truly do care and that we actually, wholeheartedly, believe that she can succeed in school. This is probably the first time in a long time that she has felt success. I definitely want that feeling to remain!

Standing with these girls also means going above and beyond what might normally be done for them in regular schools. As girls enter our program, I do everything I can to find any credit they have from other schools. These girls are proud of what they have previously earned, and they don't want to repeat those courses. I constantly check in with them and set and reset goals to make sure they can be successful. When they're ready to leave our program, I help them identify a path to follow. Some girls will change schools, do online learning, or go right into a GED program or even into another nontraditional setting. We want to do all we can to get them into a better environment academically when they leave our program.

The Best Chance to Succeed

Missy didn't succeed in public school. She thought school was mainly for socializing and that it was "uncool" to actually participate and do well. She was about a year and half behind in school when she entered our program. It took a few months for Missy to settle in and realize that school was actually important to her. After many conversations about what her future was worth, how people were standing beside her, wanting her to succeed, and how she was more than capable of doing the work needed in order to obtain her high school diploma, she started to actually believe it.

"Missy," I asked, "what do you want to do when you leave the program?"

"Well, I was thinking about going back to my regular high school."

I wasn't certain this was a good idea. "You know I want you to be in a place where you'll have the best chance to succeed. Since you've sometimes struggled in the public school environment, what do you think about a private or nontraditional school? There wouldn't be as many temptations and distractions."

Missy frowned. "Well . . . I guess that's true." She shifted her feet. "There is a school my mom told me about. It's near where I live. An

More than her words, the flicker of a smile on Missy's face told me she appreciated my help.

alternative school. But there's a lot you have to do to apply—an application, an essay, an interview—ugh!"

"Is that all?" I said. "We could definitely tackle that. I could help you get that done after school today. We could work on potential interview questions too."

Missy seemed to consider this. "Yeah," she said. "All right, let's do that." She turned to leave, then turned back again. "Um, thanks, Ms. Amanda."

More than her words, the flicker of a smile on Missy's face told me she appreciated my help.

Another way I stand with my girls is to constantly talk about their future with them. I want them to believe that they can make a new life for themselves, that they are worth more than their past has dictated, and that they have the skills and abilities to be whatever they dream they can be. For some girls that means going to college. For others it means going to a technical school to learn a trade. Whichever the case, we want each girl to know and believe that they are worth more than what they've been told, and that we will do whatever we can to help make it happen.

Finally, I stand with each of my girls by showing that I love her, that I don't judge her, and that I believe she can change. Sometimes she just needs to hear that. Sometimes she just wants someone to fight for her and continually remind her of who she truly is and who she is not. For most of her life, too many people have told her hundreds of ugly lies. It's time for her to hear the truth: that she is beautiful, smart, intelligent, worthy, creative, thoughtful, loving, kind, caring, unique—an amazing young woman.

As her teacher, I strive to stand beside her every day and tell her those things. More importantly, I strive to help her believe them for herself.

18~ The Roller-Coaster Ride to Restoration

Have you ever been in a difficult circumstance that paralyzed you—body and soul? Have you ever needed someone to open up an umbrella of love over your head, and stand with you, arm in arm, during a storm? I certainly have. When my husband left me and our baby for another woman, I faced rejection and despair. I felt like I couldn't breathe. I will always be grateful to my friend Connie, who traveled for an hour that night so that she could spread that white canopy of protection over me when I needed it most.

Connie cried with me, listened to me, and let me ask "God, why?" with absolutely no condemnation.

If you and I need a friend to stand with us during our thunderstorms, then how much more do these precious women who are trying to survive the hurricane of sex trafficking?

Over the years, we have seen the most effective recovery by our girls take place in the context of relationships. We have the credibility to help girls and women only when we offer them an authentic, ongoing connection. After all, it is only through our relationship with Jesus that we are restored to our Father. Paul reminds us that we are to be ambassadors for Christ (2 Corinthians 5:19–20)—in other words, that

> God is our constant and we are the "unstable" ones. But we must serve her like Christ and remain consistent and stable.

we are to respond to others the same way Jesus responds to us. This has to be through genuine relationship.

Authentic relationships have their ups and downs. In our relationship with God, He is our constant and we are the "unstable" ones. But when we relate to our girls and women or to anyone in crisis, we remember that since her life has been chaos, her "normal" is chaos. It's easy to overempathize and fall into a young woman's chaos, but when we do, no one is healthy. As we seek to be the constant in a person's life, we must be sure that we are connected to God, our "sure foundation" (Isaiah 33:6), so that we won't be distracted by the chaos around us.

Working through restoration with someone in crisis can be compared to riding a roller coaster. I love the story told by the grandmother in the 1989 movie *Parenthood*:

> When I was nineteen, Grandpa took me on a roller coaster. Up, down, up, down. Oh, what a ride! I always wanted to go again! You know, it is interesting to me that this ride was so frightening, so scary, so sick, so exciting, and so thrilling, all together. Some didn't like it. They went on the merry-go-round. It just goes around. Nothing. I like the roller coaster. I get more out of it.[28]

Walking with someone through crisis recovery is scary, disappointing, exciting, and thrilling. Most of the time, you feel helpless and out of control. That's where your dependence on God can flourish—and you can both get more out of it.

If we truly want to experience a deeper level of God's power, Jesus tells us that we encounter Him every time we help "the least of these" (Matthew 25:40). We encounter Him when, by God's design, our lives collide with someone who is desperate, and while we have no answers, we look intensely for God to show us *His* way.

This happens through sitting down with a person who has no hope unless God intervenes, allowing ourselves to just "be" in the situation with her. God is so faithful to show specific actions to take and words to say. Only He knows where it will lead. You see, it isn't about what you do or all the excitement of joining a compelling cause. It really is about you and God. He is the ultimate Restorer, and His work never fades.

As you can see through each of our girls' unique stories, walking with survivors of sexual abuse and trafficking is a messy and complicated opportunity. But how beautiful it is that God has given us His white umbrella of love so that we can spread it over someone in the storm. When we do that, they too can experience the love, protection, and care that Christ longs to give us all.

Notes

1. "Teen Girls' Stories of Sex Trafficking in U.S.," ABC News *Primetime*, February 9, 2006. http://abcnews.go.com/Primetime/story?id=1596778&page=1.

2. Ibid.

3. Chuck Neubauer, "Sex Trafficking in the U.S. Called 'Epidemic'," *The Washington Times*, April 23, 2011. http://www.washingtontimes.com/news/2011/apr/23/sex-trafficking-us-called-epidemic/?page=all.

4. Ibid.

5. Mary Frances Bowley, ed. Jim Lund, *A League of Dangerous Women* (Colorado Springs: Multnomah Books, 2007).

6. Sara Groves, "Eyes on the Prize." Single. Sponge Records, 2011.

7. Centers for Disease Control and Prevention. "Prevalence of Individual Adverse Childhood Experiences," last modified December 2005. http://www.cdc.gov/ace/prevalence.htm.

8. Andy Stanley, Lane Jones, and Reggie Joiner, *Seven Practices of Effective Ministry* (Colorado Springs: Multnomah Books, 2004).

9. Massachusetts Citizens for Children, "Child Sexual Abuse Questions and Answers." See www.masskids.org/index.php?option=com_content&view=article&id=150&Itemid=152.

10. Ibid.

11. Bruce D. Perry, Toi L. Blakley, Ronnie A. Pollard, William L. Baker, and Domenico Vigilante, "Childhood Trauma, the Neurobiology of Adaptation, and 'Use-dependent' Development of the Brain: How 'States' Become 'Traits.'" *Infant Mental Health Journal* 16, no. 4 (Winter 1995): 271–91. www.childtrauma.org/index.php/articles/trauma-a-ptsd/44-childhood-trauma-the-neurobiology-of-adaptation-and-quse-dependentq-development-of-the-brain-how-qstatesq-become-qtraitsq.

12. Bruce D. Perry, "Childhood Experience and the Expression of Genetic Potential: What Childhood Neglect Tells Us About Nature and Nurture," *Brain and Mind*, vol. 3 (2002): 79–100. www.childtrauma.org/index.php/articles/abuse-a-neglect.

13. Bruce D. Perry, "Examining Child Maltreatment Through a Neurodevelopmental Lens: Clinical Applications of the Neurosequential Model of Therapeutics," *Journal of Loss and Trauma*, no. 14 (2009): 240–55. http://www.childtrauma.org/index.php/articles/articles-for-professionals.

14. Bruce D. Perry and Ronnie Pollard, "Homeostasis, Stress, Trauma, and Adaptation," *Child and Adolescent Psychiatric Clinics of North America* 7, no. 1 (January 1998): 33–51. http://www.childtrauma.org/index.php/articles/articles-for-professionals.

15. Perry, "Examining Child Maltreatment Through a Neurodevelopmental Lens," *Journal of Loss and Trauma*.

16. Perry and Pollard, "Homeostasis, Stress, Trauma, and Adaptation," *Child and Adolescent Psychiatric Clinics of North America*.

17. Ibid.

18. Perry et. al., "Childhood Trauma, the Neurobiology of Adaptation, and 'Use-dependent' Development of the Brain," *Infant Mental Health Journal*.

19. Ibid.

20. Ibid.

21. Ibid.

22. John Read, Bruce D. Perry, Andrew Moskowitz, and Jan Connolly, "The Contribution of Early Traumatic Events to Schizophrenia in Some Patients," *Psychiatry* 64, no. 4 (Winter 2001): 319–45. http://www.childtrauma.org/index.php/articles/articles-for-professionals.

23. Perry and Pollard, "Homeostasis, Stress, Trauma, and Adaptation," *Child and Adolescent Psychiatric Clinics of North America*.

24. Perry et. al., "Childhood Trauma, the Neurobiology of Adaptation, and 'Use-dependent' Development of the Brain," *Infant Mental Health Journal*.

25. The Stages of Change Model was originally developed in the late 1970s and early 1980s by James Prochaska and Carlo DiClemente at the University of Rhode Island when they were studying how smokers were able to give up their habits.
Precontemplation (not yet acknowledging that there is a problem behavior that needs to be changed)
Contemplation (acknowledging that there is a problem but not yet ready or sure of wanting to make a change)
Preparation/Determination (getting ready to change)
Action/Willpower (changing behavior)
Maintenance (maintaining the behavior change) and
Relapse (returning to older behaviors and abandoning the new changes)

26. Lisa Byrd, clinical director of Wellspring Living's women's program, contributed the story about Stacy in this chapter.

27. For more about Love Gives Way in the Atlanta area, see http://lovegivesway.org.

28. *Parenthood*, directed by Ron Howard. 1989. Universal City, CA: Universal Pictures and Imagine Entertainment.

Acknowledgments

I wish to express my gratitude to the following people whom God has used in extraordinary ways to encourage the work of Wellspring Living:

My family—Dick, Matt, Mandy, Paul, Lindsay, and my mom for being a constant source of encouragement.

Lynda Dean and Helen Heard for their consistent, extravagant love shown toward the girls we serve and for their support and encouragement to our staff. My heart overflows with gratitude when I consider all you have done for me personally through the growth and development of God's work in Wellspring Living.

To Jenn McEwen and Nancy Sousa, who have become like Aaron and Hur for Wellspring Living and me personally. Your strong leadership is setting a path for God to expand His work for His girls. I am so blessed to have you by my side.

In addition, I am grateful to all the contributors in this book: Lindsay Bowley, Andy Brophy, Tracy Busse, Lisa Byrd, Bre Harper, Michelle Janicki, Amanda Johnson, Sandy Kimbrough, Sara Kincer, Jason King, Jenn McEwen, Mindy Pierce, Gina Shaw, Jeff Shaw, and Dion Stokes.

I am also grateful to Jim Lund, who has the phenomenal gift of editing and expanding stories to make them come to life for the reader. I have thoroughly enjoyed and appreciated his insight and guidance throughout this process.

Finally, I am grateful to Linda Fitzpatrick, Judy Garner, Amy Heifner, Cindy Hornaman, Gail Jeanes, Neal Kitchens, Judy Massey, Anna Marie Natale, Charlene Ray, and for the powerful prayers they have sacrificially offered on behalf of Wellspring Living over this past year and throughout the writing of this book.

Serve Locally,
Influence Globally

1 in 4 women is abused sexually by the time she reaches adulthood. In 2001, Wellspring Living was formed to help survivors of childhood sexual abuse overcome their broken pasts and move toward hopeful futures.

Our mission is to confront the issue of childhood sexual abuse and exploitation through advocacy, education, and treatment programs for girls and women. Our programs are a refuge for women and girls who need a chance to start over.

Wellspring Living strategies include:

- Offering survivors a safe haven where they receive therapy, personalized education, life skills, and spiritual renewal
- Advocating for victims — give a voice to the voiceless and confront the issue of sexual exploitation
- Sharing best practices with others by training organizations assisting in building programs to serve survivors of childhood sexual abuse and exploitation

Wellspring Living desires to embody servant leadership, unrelenting compassion, community building, comprehensive service, excellence in care, sensitive faith, and stewardship to all we serve.

wellspringliving.org   **Wellspring Living** Rescue. Restore. Renew.   thewhiteumbrellacampaign.com

WARNING SIGNS:

TRAITS OF TRAFFICKING

- Significantly older boyfriend
- Signs of trauma (physical or other)
- Travel with older male (not guardian)
- Chronic runaway
- Multiple delinquent charges
- Homelessness
- Special marked tattoos
- Substance abuse

* Shared Hope International (Sharedhope.org)

MINISTERING TO VICTIMS
OF SEXUAL EXPLOITATION

The Moody Bible Institute now offers a unique
bachelor's degree program to train students in
ministering to victims of sex crimes, sex trafficking,
and all other forms of sexual exploitation or abuse.

The B.A. program will prepare students for ministry
of advocacy and restoration to those who are the
victims of sexual exploitation. This preparation
combines thorough biblical training and strategic
partnership with skilled ministry practitioners such
as Wellspring Living. Students spend the summer
after their junior year, and the fall semester of their
senior year, in ministry immersion.

**For more information about this exciting
new opportunity, please visit www.moody.edu.**